100 Great Breads
Paul Hollywood

Photographs by Neil Barclay

CASSELL
ILLUSTRATED

First published in Great Britain in 2004 by Cassell Illustrated,
a division of Octopus Publishing Group Limited,
2-4 Heron Quays, London E14 4JP

Copyright © 2004 Paul Hollywood

A CIP catalogue record for this book is available from the
British Library.

ISBN 1 84403 143 8
EAN 9781844031436

Edited by Victoria Alers-Hankey and Barbara Dixon
Photographs by Neil Barclay
Styled by Fanny Ward
Design by DW Design
Jacket design by Jo Knowles

Printed in China

Acknowledgements

This book is dedicated to my wife, Alexandra, and my special boy, Joshua.

I would like to thank my mother, Gill, and father, John, for encouraging me into the baking trade in the first place and for washing endless mountains of chef's whites. I'd also like to thank my mother-in-law, Gloria, for helping me with some great recipe ideas.

Above all, a special thank you to my wife, Alexandra, for her support, love and patience during my career and the writing of this book.

Contents

Introduction

Bread is the one natural food that has been with us for centuries, but in recent years it has taken a back seat while we indulged our passion for fast foods bursting with additives and E numbers.

I grew up in Liverpool, the oldest of three boys, and food to us was just a source of energy. It wasn't until I began to make bread in my father's bakery that I realized that the variations and different types of bread were endless and that bread was not just the thick, white, sliced stuff to make bacon butties with!

The aroma of freshly baked bread evokes feelings and memories in all of us – a snug kitchen in the winter after school and a still-warm loaf on the table waiting to be smothered in butter and home-made strawberry jam is one of my favourites, but who can resist ciabatta straight from the oven, stuffed with glossy black olives, garlic and fresh coriander? Close your eyes and you're sitting on a vine-covered, sun-drenched terrace, sipping a glass of rich, red wine and surrounded by friends and family.

All the recipes in this book have special memories for me; some are from my childhood and some were discovered during my travels abroad. The textures and flavours all vary greatly, reflecting their origins, and I have added something of myself to all these recipes to make them unique and, I hope, satisfying to recreate.

Baking bread is a very sociable experience – you will find the whole family crowding into your kitchen, drawn by the irresistible fragrance of salmon brioche or a potato and rosemary focaccia. So pull up the chairs, break open a bottle and enjoy the novel experience of eating a home-baked loaf of bread.

The History of Bread

I am a man who has bread in Heliopolis
My bread is in heaven with the Sun God,
My bread is on earth with Keb.

The bark of evening and of morning
Brings me the bread that is my meat
From the house of the Sun God.

(Book Of The Dead, Ancient Egypt*)*

From the depths of time bread has been the one common factor that has linked the world's cultures together.

A recent excavation in Egypt, two miles south of the Sphinx, revealed an ancient bakery, complete with moulds and working tools of the day. Meanwhile in London, builders working along the banks of the River Thames unearthed ancient loaves of bread dating back to Roman times.

The first breads made were dense and unappealing – the grain was crushed and mixed with water to create a gruel, which was then left over a fire to cook hard. They were ideal for early man, being easy to carry on the hunt or into battle, and they would keep for days at a time, but they were not very appetizing.

It was the ancient Egyptians who took baking 10 steps further. They discovered that the crushed grain and water mush, if left in a warm and moist atmosphere, would produce bubbles – the first sign of risen bread. This, mixed with fresh flour and then baked, would produce an aerated bread – and so the first yeast was created. Bread was incredibly important to the Egyptians. The lower classes lived almost exclusively on bread and it was used

as a form of payment by the Pharaohs for work done on the pyramids and temples. Today's Egyptians still eat their meat or vegetables stuffed into loaves of bread, rather like a kebab.

The people of Israel were influenced by their contact with the Egyptians and began to produce a bread of their own. Theirs was a nomadic society, so until they settled, they baked their dough in the ashes of fires, producing a flat, cake-like bread. Later on they began to build ovens and granaries, some of which, like the hill fortress of Masada, are still visible today.

The Greeks began by importing their corn from Egypt, but later began to cultivate their own crops. Grain equalled power in Ancient Greece, land owners were eligible for high offices when a certain standard of productivity was obtained, and in the 7th century BC the 'Party of Bread' – the most prosperous farmers – ruled Athens.

The Roman Empire also imported their flour from overseas, from such places as Egypt and North Africa and the Romans were responsible for the introduction of the water mill. These entrepreneurs had also developed elegant tastes and many of the breads made then would be acceptable today – sesame seed bread, almond bread and milk bread, to name but a few. After the Roman Empire eventually collapsed, it appears that even as late as the 5th century, many Europeans were still making their bread at home.

The art of bread making progressed slowly during the Dark Ages and baking remained a family task in the villages and countryside for many hundreds of years. Eventually, communal ovens were introduced and, for a fee, bakers baked off the bread that was brought in. Some of these communal ovens are still currently in operation in France, where they consider the practice of bread making to be an art form.

Today, there are still people all over the world who bake their bread daily. The Bedouin in Petra, Jordan, bake on a bakestone, the modern version of which is a metal dome, lightly oiled and set over a flame. In some European countries families still come together to bake bread and make it a social occasion, and some even have specially made ovens in their back gardens for just such an event.

Bread holds a social, religious and gastronomic significance for all of us, but it is not just the act of breaking the bread that we should honour, but also the act of making or creating the bread.

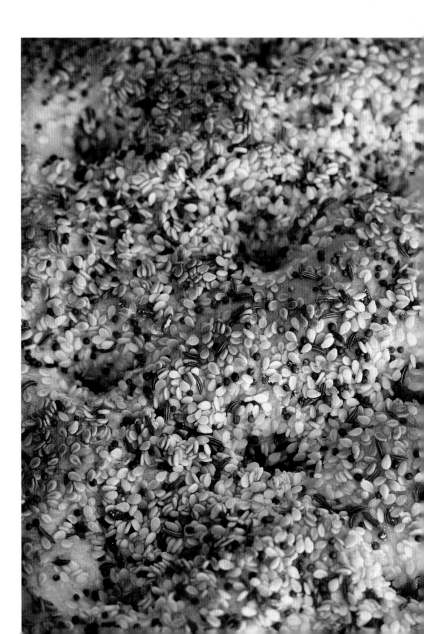

Tools, Techniques and Tips

Tools

There are only a few tools needed to make a good loaf:

1. Baking trays and loaf tins

Any 450 g/1 lb traditional loaf tin is ideal for making breads. There are several varieties available, from Teflon to non-stick; some tins have straight sides, while others, such as farmhouse tins, tend to be more rounded.

Do remember to grease the tins – I use olive oil – before putting the dough in as this will ensure that the bread doesn't stick.

Baking trays are lined throughout – I line my trays with silicone paper or baking parchment. Greaseproof paper tends to stick.

2. Ovens

I have made bread in or on every oven imaginable, from open-flame to fan-assisted to range cookers; all are great for baking bread. Every oven has a character, especially in professional bakeries, and hot spots are common. Be aware of your oven as it may have these elusive hotspots; use them when baking and remember to turn your bread if the oven is a little hot at the back – the main reason for ovens being especially hot at the back is because over-impatient bakers look in the oven too often.

Most of the recipes in this book need oven temperatures between 200°–220°C/400°–425°F/mark 6–7. This is more than enough heat to bake bread; most industrial bakeries bake at 250°C/475°F/mark 9+, the main reason being to keep moisture in the loaf. The longer a loaf takes to colour or bake the drier it will be.

3. A good serrated knife or a sharp blade

I have no preferences with the knives that I use – any will do, but just remember to keep them sharp: the cut on the bread is very important, not only for the look, but for the crumb texture.

Techniques

Yeast

There are two main types of yeast available in the supermarkets today – dried and instant. Using dried yeast makes more work for yourself because you have to add water and sugar and leave it to froth. Instant yeast is more user-friendly because you literally throw it straight into the flour. However, be aware that this is a concentrated yeast and you will need less of it. All the recipes in this book use fresh yeast, but I would suggest you use instant yeast if you can't obtain fresh – if you use instant or dried then use 25 per cent less than the recipe states. Fresh yeast is available from most supermarkets nowadays – ask at the bakery department for a small amount and more often than not they will sell it to you. Failing that, ask at your local bakery.

Remember: all recipes use fresh yeast, so if you are using instant or dried yeast, reduce the quantities a little.

Mixing the ingredients for the dough

When mixing the ingredients, avoid contact between the yeast and salt: salt kills yeast, which means the bread won't rise.

Kneading

Kneading is an important part of bread making. The way I knead is very simple: start by making an indentation with the palms of your

hands into the middle of the dough – not too deep – then lift up the dough at the top and press it into the hole you have just made. Turn the dough and repeat and keep repeating this process for the length of time stated in the recipe. The kneading times I give may fluctuate by 2 minutes each way as you get more proficient.

Adding flavourings to the dough

Always add any flavourings after the dough has been kneaded and rested for at least 1 hour as this helps the dough to stabilize before being pumped with any additions.

When adding ingredients such as onions and garlic – ingredients that are intrinsically acidic – do not add too much as this retards or slows down the rising of the dough.

Tips

- Use this book as a base, but try incorporating your own ingredients and experiment with flavours and textures.

- You do not always need to dissolve yeast in warm water, just lob it in.

- You do not always need to use warm water when making bread, the bread will rise anyway, even in the fridge. The slower the rising (proving) time the more flavour the bread will have.

- The recipes in this book have measured water contents, but flours differ, so you may need a little extra water or a little less.

- When rolling out and kneading the dough, do not coat the table in inches of flour. The dough will pick it up and tighten up too much.

- I do not normally cover the dough when it is resting; a little skinning on the top should be incorporated back into the dough.

- Always preheat your oven so that your bread has somewhere to go when it is ready and not you!

- None of the breads in this book require steam or pots of water in the oven, I like the crusty earthy look of home-baked bread – there's nothing better.

- I put most of my breads onto a cooling rack when they come out of the oven – this is to prevent the bread from sweating and going soft.

- Do not store baked bread in a fridge – it will go stale three times quicker than if left in a bread bin.

To help you with the skills needed to make bread, your first task is to make a wheatsheaf loaf, which is a display bread and is pictured on page 9. If you can make a wheatsheaf you can make anything in this book. Before you begin, read the tips on the previous pages.

750 g/1 lb 10 oz strong white
flour, plus extra for dusting
60 g/2½ oz salt
5 g/¼ oz fresh yeast
60 ml/2 fl oz olive oil
420 ml/14½ fl oz water
1 egg, beaten, for eggwash

Wheatsheaf Loaf

1. Put the flour in a bowl about 30.5 cm/ 12 inches in diameter, then add the salt to the left and the yeast to the right. This is to avoid contact between the yeast and the salt (remember, salt kills yeast on contact, which means the bread won't rise). Although you do not need to avoid contact between the two when making a wheatsheaf, it is a good practice to get into.

2. Add the olive oil and slowly start to add the water. (It's not necessary to use virgin olive oil since a lot of the flavour of the oil will be lost during baking.)

3. Begin squeezing the mixture together in your hands. Your aim is to pick up all the flour in the bowl with the water – you may need a little extra or a little less water. What you are looking for is a soft, pliable dough.

4. Now shape the dough roughly into a ball and tip it out onto a lightly floured surface. (I say lightly floured because most people make the fatal error of adding too much flour and tightening up the dough too much, and what started as a perfect dough ends up like a brick.)

5. Now you can begin kneading (see pages 12–13). Turn the dough 45 degrees and make another indentation and fold in the top of the dough. Repeat this process for 10 minutes. With practice you will eventually get quicker. Put the dough back in the bowl to rest for 1 hour. This is to allow the dough to relax and the yeast to activate.

6. Rip off about a quarter of the dough and, using a rolling pin, roll it out to a rectangle, about 45.5 cm/18 inches long and 1 cm/½ inch thick – use a little flour to stop the rolling pin from attaching itself to the dough.

Wheatsheaf Loaf (continued)

7. Using a knife, cut out a keyhole, or wheatsheaf, shape from the dough, about 45.5 cm/18 inches long and 20.5 cm/ 8 inches across at the top, round end. Using the dough trimmings and extra dough, hand-roll out 20–30 pieces about 20.5 cm/8 inches long and as thin as you can get them. (When rolling dough, the trick is to use the full length of your hand, from your fingertips to your palms.)

8. To plait the dough, spread three strands in front of you and join them at the top. Cross the left one over the middle strand to the right and the right one over the middle strand to the left, then repeat until you have plaited the whole length.

9. Line a baking tray with silicone paper and put the keyhole dough on it. Carefully raise the round end of the wheatsheaf dough and place the plait under it at the bottom, with the excess laid out on either side. Press firmly to flatten out the dough underneath.

10. Brush the straight length with a little water, then begin adding the hand-rolled strands from the top of the straight length down to the bottom, to simulate the stems of the corn. When the base is covered, trim off any overhanging bits at the bottom, reroll them and use to make a long-tailed mouse. Place the mouse towards the bottom of the stems of corn.

11. Next, rip off small pieces of dough and roll into balls, then slightly elongate them. Brush the round head of the dough with a little water. Place a row of balls to just overlap the top edge of the strips on the straight length, then add a row above. Fold in the two ends of the plait onto where the strips of dough meet the balls and press lightly to seal. Place balls all around the edge of the round head, then fill in the centre with rows of balls just overlapping the previous row. Leave the wheatsheaf to rest for 1 hour, to allow it to rise slightly.

12. Preheat the oven to 200°C/400°F/mark 6. Brush the wheatsheaf with the eggwash – this gives the baked bread a beautiful golden shine – and bake for 30 minutes. Lower the temperature to 150°C/300°F/mark 2 and bake for 30 minutes more. Cool on a wire rack.

Basic Breads

Remember to use a little olive oil to grease your loaf tins. Apply it with a cloth or a spray gun.

This bread, which dates back to medieval times, was known as one of the oven bottoms, as this was invariably where it was baked (as is the Farl on page 31). Baked to a deep colour, it's a great British loaf – I remember watching my dad moulding these when I was a kid.

White Bread

Crusty Cob

500 g/1 lb 2 oz strong white flour, plus extra for dusting

1 tablespoon salt

60 ml/2 fl oz olive oil

20 g/¾ oz yeast

270 ml/9 fl oz water

Makes 1 x 450 g/ 1 lb loaf

Mix all the ingredients in a large bowl, taking care not to put the yeast on top of the salt. Knead well with your hands and knuckles, then leave to rise for 1 hour.

Oil a 450 g/1 lb loaf tin. Tip the dough out onto a lightly floured surface and mould into a sausage shape. Put back in the tin and leave to rise for 30 minutes–1 hour.

Preheat the oven to 230°C/450°F/ mark 8. Dust the top of the dough with flour, put the tin in the oven and bake for 35 minutes.

Take out of the oven and turn the loaf out onto a wire rack to cool.

500 g/1 lb 2 oz strong white flour, plus extra for dusting

1 tablespoon salt

30 g/1 oz yeast

40 g/1½ oz butter, softened

300 ml/½ pint water

Makes 1 x 450 g/ 1 lb loaf

Put the flour, salt, yeast and butter into a large bowl and mix together. Add nearly all the water and blend the ingredients together, then add the remaining water and mix in the bowl for 2 minutes.

Tip the dough out onto a lightly floured surface and knead well for 5 minutes, then place the dough back in the bowl and leave to rest for 2 hours.

Line a baking tray. Shape the dough into a ball, place on the baking tray and leave to rise for 1 hour.

Preheat the oven to 220°C/425°F/ mark 7. Using a sharp knife, slash the dough across the top and dust with flour. Bake for 30 minutes until golden brown, then transfer to a wire rack to cool.

A very old British recipe, mainly baked around Georgian times when white flour was prevalent. This sweet white loaf was favoured by the upper crust of this country!

The ubiquitous loaf the Brits have brought to the table. But I shouldn't mock, made well this is a beautiful bread – served as toast or as a simple sandwich it's magic! The main recipe is for white bread, but try the wholemeal version to help you understand the different textures.

Batch Bread

White (or Wholemeal) Tin Bread

500 g/1 lb 2 oz strong white flour, plus extra for dusting

1½ teaspoons salt

30 g/1 oz yeast

60 g/2½ oz butter, softened

75 g/3 oz caster sugar

300 ml/½ pint water

Makes 1 loaf

Put all the ingredients into a large bowl and mix together. When all the flour has been picked up by the water, tip the dough out onto a lightly floured surface and knead for 5 minutes. If you find the dough sticks a lot to the table, then dust lightly again with flour, but do not over-flour as this will tighten the dough. Put the dough back in the bowl and leave to rest for 1 hour.

Line a baking tray. Tip the dough out onto your floured surface and shape into a ball, then gently flatten it out with your hand until it is about 20.5 cm/8 inches in diameter. Dust the top with flour, place on the baking tray and leave to rise for 1–2 hours.

Preheat the oven to 200°C/400°F/mark 6. Bake the loaf for 15–20 minutes, then transfer to a wire rack to cool.

500 g/1 lb 2 oz strong white flour, plus extra for dusting

1 tablespoon salt

30 g/1 oz yeast

50 g/2 oz butter, softened

290 ml/9½ fl oz water

Makes 1 x 900 g/ 2 lb loaf or 2 x 450 g/1 lb loaves

Put the flour, salt, yeast and butter into a bowl, then add the water, little by little, folding in with your hands until all the flour has been picked up. Tip out onto a lightly floured surface and knead for 5 minutes until you have a pliable, soft dough. Put the dough back in the bowl and leave for 1 hour.

Oil the loaf tin or tins. Shape the dough to fit the tin(s), and leave to rise for 1 hour.

Preheat the oven to 230°C/450°F/mark 8. Just before you bake the loaf, dust the top with flour and, using a knife, make slashes across the top. Bake for 30–35 minutes, then turn out of the tin(s) onto a wire rack to cool.

Variation: For Wholemeal Tin Bread use 400 g/14 oz wholemeal flour and 100 g/3½ oz white flour instead of the 500 g/1 lb 2 oz white flour, and use 320 ml/11 fl oz of water. Proceed as above.

Wholemeal flour does take more water than white flour. If you find that your particular flour needs more water than the quantity given, then by all means add more. Make the dough quite wet, because as the dough rests it does tighten up.

This bread is a very British shape. It originated some time around the 1500s and still exists in small village bakeries around the country.

Basic Wholemeal Bread

100 g/3½ oz strong white flour, plus extra for dusting

400 g/14 oz wholemeal flour

1½ teaspoons salt

30 g/1 oz yeast

50 g/2 oz butter, softened

345 ml/12 fl oz water

Makes 1 loaf

Put the flours, salt, yeast and butter into a large bowl and mix together. Slowly add the water, mixing with your hand until all the flour has been incorporated from the sides of the bowl.

Tip the dough out onto a lightly floured surface and knead for 5–7 minutes. Put the dough back in the bowl and leave to rest for 1 hour.

Preheat the oven to 220°C/425°F/ mark 7. Line a baking tray. Using a knife, cut a slash down the middle on top of the dough and dust the top with flour. Bake for 30 minutes, then transfer to a wire rack to cool.

Cottage Loaf

400 g/14 oz strong white flour, plus extra for dusting

1½ teaspoons salt

30 g/1 oz yeast

60 g/2½ oz butter, softened

250 ml/8½ fl oz water

Makes 1 loaf

Put all the ingredients into a bowl and mix until you have a soft, pliable dough.

Tip the dough out onto a lightly floured surface and knead with your fingers for 5 minutes, then put back in the bowl and rest the dough for 1 hour.

Preheat the oven to 230°C/450°F/ mark 8. Tip the dough out onto your floured surface, rip off a third of the dough and shape into a ball. Shape the remaining dough into a ball and place the smaller ball on top of the larger, then flatten slightly with your hand. Push your finger down through the centre of the loaf from top to bottom until you can feel the table. Dust the loaf with flour and, using a knife, make vertical slashes from the top of the loaf to the bottom (be careful not to cut yourself).

Put onto a lined baking tray and bake for 30 minutes until golden brown. Transfer to a wire rack to cool.

When cooled, serve with chunks of cheese.

A friend started me on this – it was his birthday and he asked me if he could see his name in bread – better than in lights! These baked letters are not for eating, but for display only.

A very ancient bread. Milk has been used in bread for at least 1,500 years and it gives a characteristic flavour and a fairly tight texture.

Named Bread

500 g/1 lb 2 oz strong white flour, plus extra for dusting

50 g/2 oz salt

5 g/¼ oz yeast

30 ml/1 fl oz olive oil

270 ml/9 fl oz water

1 egg, beaten, for eggwash

wood varnish, to glaze

Makes 400 small letters

Put all the ingredients into a bowl and mix well by rubbing in. Tip the dough out onto a lightly floured surface and knead for 6 minutes, then put the dough back in the bowl to rest for 1 hour.

Line several baking trays. Divide the dough into however many letters you require, e.g. Paul needs 4, so cut 4 x 100 pieces of dough, and shape the dough into the required letters. Put the letters on the baking tray so they are just touching, and leave to rest for 1 hour.

Preheat the oven to 220°C/425°F/ mark 7. Brush the letters liberally with eggwash, put in the oven and bake for 30–40 minutes until they are a strong dark brown.

Transfer onto a wire rack to cool. The following day, coat the names with wood varnish to preserve them.

Milk Loaf

500 g/1 lb 2 oz strong white flour, plus extra for dusting

1½ teaspoons salt

50 g/2 oz caster sugar

60 g/2½ oz butter, softened

30 g/1 oz yeast

300 ml/½ pint milk

Makes 2 x 450 g/ 1 lb loaves

Put all the ingredients into a large bowl. Using a mixer, begin blending slowly, then speed up as you start to pick up all the flour. Alternatively, mix by hand.

Tip the dough out onto a lightly floured surface and knead for 5 minutes. Put the dough back in the bowl and leave to rise until doubled in size.

Tip the dough out onto your floured surface and divide into two pieces. Shape each piece roughly into a sausage shape and place crease-side down into two 450 g/ 1 lb loaf tins. Leave to rise for 1 hour.

Preheat the oven to 200°C/400°F/ mark 6. Bake the loaves for 25–30 minutes until golden brown, then turn out onto a wire rack to cool.

This earthy, hearty, full-flavoured loaf is from Eastern Europe. It will take up to 30 per cent more water than most bread doughs. The recipe uses rye baskets – they can be bought in basketware shops or ordered through the Internet.

I've tweaked this recipe over the years and am finally proud of it. It's gorgeous served fresh from the oven with lots of butter.

Dark Rye Bread *Illustrated*

Irish Soda Bread

350 g/12 oz dark rye flour, plus extra for dusting

150 g/5 oz wholemeal flour

1½ teaspoons salt

30 g/1 oz yeast

4 tablespoons malt extract

2 tablespoons treacle

385 ml/13½ fl oz water

2 teaspoons cumin seeds

Makes 2 small loaves

Put 175 g/6 oz of rye flour and 75 g/3 oz of wholemeal flour into a bowl, then stir in the salt, yeast, malt extract and treacle and 150 ml/¼ pint of the water. Mix well for 5 minutes, then leave in the bowl to rise for 5 hours.

Line a baking tray. Add the remaining flours and water and the cumin seeds to the dough and mix well. Tip out onto a lightly floured surface, divide the dough into two and shape each into an oblong sausage. Coat each sausage with rye flour, place each in a rye basket and leave to rise for 2–3 hours.

Preheat the oven to 220°C/425°F/mark 7. Tip each loaf out onto the baking tray and bake in the oven for 35 minutes, then transfer to a wire rack to cool.

500 g/1 lb 2 oz strong white flour, plus extra for dusting

20 g/¾ oz baking powder

1 teaspoon salt

75 g/3 oz butter, softened

150 ml/¼ pint buttermilk

150 ml/¼ pint milk

2 medium eggs, beaten

Makes 2 loaves

Put the flour, baking powder and salt into a bowl and work in the butter. Stir in the remaining ingredients and mix well.

Line a baking tray. Combine the mixture with your hands to make a dough, then divide the dough into two and shape into balls. Flatten the balls out and cut crosses in the top of each, then put on the baking tray and leave to rest for 20 minutes.

Preheat the oven to 200°C/400°F/mark 6. Dust the dough lightly with flour and bake in the oven for 30–40 minutes. Transfer to a wire rack to cool.

I first ate this bread, baked for me by monks, while staying in Roscrea Monastery in Ireland.

A nice twist on the traditional bread, and tastes fantastic!

Wholemeal Soda Bread *Illustrated*

250 g/9 oz strong white flour, plus extra for dusting

250 g/9 oz wholemeal flour

20 g/¾ oz baking powder

40 g/1½ oz caster sugar

75 g/3 oz butter, softened

270 ml/9 fl oz milk

30 ml/1 fl oz buttermilk

Makes 1 loaf

Preheat the oven to 200°C/400°F/ mark 6. Line a baking tray. Put all the ingredients into a large bowl and work together to form a soft dough. Shape into a ball and flatten slightly and cut a cross into the top, then dust the top with a little flour.

Put onto the baking tray and bake for 25 minutes until golden brown. Transfer to a wire rack to cool.

Variation: This bread can be made with 100 per cent white flour – just replace the wholemeal flour with 250 g/9 oz of white flour. Proceed as above.

Cheese and Onion Soda Bread

500 g/1 lb 2 oz strong white flour, plus extra for dusting

1½ teaspoons salt

300 ml/½ pint buttermilk

30 g/1 oz caster sugar

75 g/3 oz butter, softened

20 g/¾ oz baking powder

1 onion, peeled and finely chopped

75 g/3 oz Cheddar cheese, grated

Makes 2 loaves

Preheat the oven to 220°C/425°F/ mark 7. Line a baking tray. Put all the ingredients except the onion and cheese in a food mixer and, using a paddle blade and medium speed, blend together for 2 minutes. Alternatively, put into a bowl and mix well by hand for 5 minutes. Add the onion and cheese and incorporate, either by hand or in the mixer (don't overmix), into the dough.

Divide the dough into two pieces and tip out onto a lightly floured surface. Shape each piece into a ball, then flatten each with your hand so they are approximately 5 cm/2 inches thick. Cut a deep cross into each, dust with a little flour and put on the baking tray.

Bake for 30 minutes, then serve warm.

Not that I drink a lot of beer (I prefer lager), but this bread is delicious! Serve with a good mature Cheddar cheese.

Another hearty loaf, with a little extra iron (i.e. Guinness). Eat yourself fit!

Beer Bread

Guinness and Treacle Bread

250 g/9 oz wholemeal flour

250 g/9 oz strong white flour, plus extra for dusting

1 tablespoon salt

20 g/¾ oz yeast

30 g/1 oz butter, softened

300 ml/½ pint good beer

Makes 1 loaf

Put all the ingredients into a bowl and mix until all the flour has been picked up. Tip the dough out onto a lightly floured surface and knead for 5 minutes until the dough is smooth and creamy. Put the dough back into the bowl to rest for 1 hour.

Line a baking tray. Tip the dough out onto your floured surface and shape into a ball, then flatten out with your hands and cut diagonal lines across the top. Put the dough on the baking tray and leave to rise for 1 hour.

Preheat the oven to 200°C/400°F/ mark 6. Bake the loaf for 30 minutes until golden brown, then transfer to a wire rack to cool.

350 g/12 oz wholemeal flour, plus extra for dusting

150 g/5 oz strong white flour, plus extra for dusting

1 tablespoon salt

30 g/1 oz yeast

2 tablespoons treacle

150 ml/¼ pint Guinness

120 ml/4 fl oz water

Makes 1 loaf

Put all the ingredients into a large bowl and mix together for a few minutes. Tip the dough out onto a lightly floured surface and knead for 5 minutes, then put the dough back in the bowl and leave to rest for 1 hour.

Line a baking tray. Tip the dough out onto your floured surface and shape into a ball, then flatten and roll up. Put the dough on the baking tray and leave to rise for 1 hour.

Preheat the oven to 200°C/400°F/ mark 6. Cut several slashes across the bread and dust with wholemeal flour. Bake for 30 minutes, then transfer to a wire rack to cool.

This bread is an old favourite of mine, originally created for the Michelin-starred restaurant at the Dorchester. Serve as a sandwich, piled high with crisp green salad, roasted red and yellow peppers and slivers of mustard-roasted beef. You need to start this the day before.

This multi-flavoured and coloured bread is ideal for indecisive families – there are rolls of four flavours in each loaf. It's great for dinner parties, too. The dough can be frozen when made, if not using immediately, and then defrosted overnight before baking.

Stilton and Bacon Bread

Multi-flavoured Bread

500 g/1 lb 2 oz strong white flour, plus extra for dusting

500 ml/17 fl oz water

20 g/¾ oz yeast

1½ teaspoons salt

75 g/3 oz Stilton cheese, crumbled

125 g/4 oz bacon, chopped and fried

Makes 2 loaves

Put 125 g/4 oz of the flour, 120 ml/ 4 fl oz of the water and 15 g/½ oz of the yeast into a bowl and mix together by hand, then whisk with a hand whisk for 5 minutes. Leave to rise in a warm place overnight.

The dough will now smell fermented, rather like beer. Add the remaining flour, water and yeast and the salt and knead well for 5 minutes, then leave to rest for 30 minutes.

Line a baking tray. Tip the dough out onto a lightly floured surface and divide into two pieces. Add half the Stilton and half the bacon into each piece, then shape them into two rounds, put on the baking tray and leave to prove for 1 hour.

Preheat the oven to 200°C/400°F/ mark 6. Dust the loaves with flour and bake for 30 minutes, then transfer to a wire rack to cool.

½ quantity Curried Naan Bread dough (see page 73)

½ quantity Date and Fig Bread dough (see page 104)

½ quantity Pepper and Onion Flowerpot Bread dough (see page 88)

½ quantity Stilton and Walnut Wholemeal Loaf dough (see page 103)

For the toppings

sesame seeds

poppy seeds

flour

grated cheese

Makes 3–4 loaves

Line 2 baking trays. Make the doughs and divide them into 100 g/3½ oz pieces, then shape them into balls.

Place one ball of dough on the tray and surround with 5 balls of different flavours. Make similar circles with the remaining balls, then leave to rise for 1 hour. The individual circles of dough will join up to form loaves.

Preheat the oven to 200°C/400°F/ mark 6. Bake for 25 minutes, then transfer to a wire rack to cool. Et voila – multi flavours!

This bread is a very English loaf, traditionally baked on the bottom of the oven, hence its other name: oven bottoms!

These rolls are great for dinner parties – with three flavours to choose from, there's one to appeal to everyone.

Farl *Illustrated*

Mixed Rolls

500 g/1 lb 2 oz strong white flour, plus extra for dusting

1 tablespoon salt

30 g/1 oz yeast

60 g/2½ oz butter, softened

300 ml/½ pint water

Makes 1 large loaf

Put all the ingredients into a bowl and mix for 4 minutes. Tip out onto a lightly floured surface and knead for 5 minutes until the dough is smooth and pliable. Leave in the bowl to rise for 1 hour.

Line a baking tray. Tip the dough out onto your floured surface and shape into a ball, then flatten into a circle about 5 cm/2 inches thick. Put on the baking tray and leave to rise for 1 hour.

Preheat the oven to 220°C/425°F/mark 7. Cover the top of the dough with flour and, starting from the middle, make vertical slashes down the dough all the way round. Bake in the oven for 30 minutes, then transfer to a wire rack to cool.

For the dough

500 g/1 lb 2 oz strong white flour, plus extra for dusting

1 tablespoon salt

60 g/2½ oz butter, softened

30 g/1 oz yeast

300 ml/½ pint water

For the flavourings

20 g/¾ oz red or green peppers, deseeded and finely chopped, and 20 g/¾ oz onion, peeled and finely chopped

20 g/¾ oz Stilton, crumbled, and 30 g/1 oz chopped walnuts

75 g/3 oz Brie, chopped, and a good handful freshly chopped basil

Makes 15–20 rolls

Put all the ingredients for the dough into a bowl and mix until all the flour has been picked up. Tip the dough out onto a lightly floured surface and knead for 5 minutes, then put the dough back in the bowl and leave to rest for 1 hour.

Line baking trays and dust with a little flour. Divide the dough into three pieces. Incorporate the peppers and onions into one piece and divide into 75 g/3 oz balls. Place on a baking tray, then cut a cross on the top of each one.

Incorporate the Stilton and walnuts into the second piece of dough, then divide the dough into 75 g/3 oz pieces. Roll each into a sausage and tie in a knot, then place on a baking tray.

Roll out the remaining piece of dough into a rectangle 1 cm/½ inch thick and scatter the top with the Brie and basil. Starting from the long side, roll up the rectangle and press lightly on the edge to seal. Cut through the sausage every 5 cm/2 inches and place each piece, cut-side down, on a baking tray. Leave all the rolls to rise for 1 hour.

Preheat the oven to 220°C/425°F/mark 7. Bake the rolls for 20 minutes, then transfer to a wire rack to cool.

A traditional afternoon tea favourite, served with clotted cream and strawberry jam. I've worked in several five-star hotels and, as far as I'm concerned, afternoon tea is the best snack of the day – especially at Cliveden.

These are a particular favourite of a friend of mine, Chris Davies, who insisted I put the recipe in the book. If preferred you may add 50 g/ 2 oz sultanas to the dough when it has been formed.

Scones *Illustrated*

Wholemeal Scones

500 g/1 lb 2 oz strong white flour, plus extra for dusting

2 medium eggs, beaten, plus 1 egg, beaten, for eggwash

75 g/3 oz caster sugar

30 g/1 oz baking powder

75 g/3 oz butter, softened

230 ml/8 fl oz milk

100 g/3½ oz sultanas

Makes 15–18 scones

Preheat the oven to 220°C/425°F/ mark 7. Line a baking tray.

Put all the ingredients except the eggwash and sultanas into a food mixer and, using a paddle blade, mix for about 2 minutes on slow speed. If mixing by hand this will take about 5 minutes.

Incorporate the sultanas into the dough and tip out onto a lightly floured surface. Using a rolling pin, roll out the dough to about 5 cm/2 inches thick, then, using a round cutter, cut out the scones. (I normally use a 5–7.5 cm/ 2–3 inch cutter for the hotel-size scone.)

Put the scones on the baking tray and brush with the eggwash. If you've the time, chill the eggwashed scones in the fridge for 30 minutes before baking to help with a straight rise.

Remove the scones from the fridge and brush the tops again with eggwash, being careful not to let it dribble down the sides as this will hinder their rise in the oven. Bake for 15 minutes, then transfer to a wire rack to cool a little. Serve warm.

250 g/9 oz strong white flour, plus extra for dusting

250 g/9 oz wholemeal flour

75 g/3 oz caster sugar

30 g/1 oz baking powder

75 g/3 oz butter, softened

2 medium eggs, beaten, plus 1 egg, beaten, for eggwash

270 ml/9 fl oz milk

Makes 15–18 scones

Preheat the oven to 200°C/400°F/ mark 6. Line a baking tray.

Put the flours, sugar and baking powder into a large bowl and mix together.

Add the butter, eggs and milk and, using your hands, mix together thoroughly for 6 minutes.

Turn the dough out onto a lightly floured surface and, using a rolling pin, flatten it to about 5 cm/2 inches thick. Using a round cutter (any size you like – I prefer to use 5–7.5 cm/2–3 inch cutters), cut out the scones.

Put the scones on the baking tray and brush with the eggwash. If you've the time, chill the eggwashed scones in the fridge for 30 minutes before baking to help with a straight rise.

Remove the scones from the fridge and brush the tops again with eggwash, being careful not to let it dribble down the sides as this will hinder their rise in the oven. Bake for 15–20 minutes until golden brown, then transfer to a wire rack to cool a little. Serve cool with strawberry jam.

Cheese and scones is a marriage made in heaven. You can add 30 g/
1 oz of sultanas to the dough if you like.

Cheese Scones

500 g/1 lb 2 oz strong
white flour, plus extra
for dusting

30 g/1 oz caster sugar

30 g/1 oz baking
powder

75 g/3 oz butter,
softened

2 eggs, beaten
together, plus 1 egg,
beaten, for eggwash

240 ml/8 fl oz milk

100 g/3½ oz Cheddar
cheese, grated

Makes 15 scones

Line a baking tray. Put the flour, sugar, baking powder, butter, the
2 beaten eggs and the milk into a bowl and bring together gently with
your hands. When the dough has formed, add most of the cheese
(reserving a little for sprinkling) and mix again for 5 minutes.

Tip the dough out onto a lightly floured surface and knead gently for
4 minutes until the dough is smooth. Roll out the dough to 4 cm/
1½ inches thick and, using a cutter size of your choice, cut out the
scones. Put the scones on the baking tray, brush the tops with the
eggwash and put in the fridge for 30 minutes (this helps the scone to
rise up straight).

Preheat the oven to 220°C/425°F/mark 7. Remove the scones from the
fridge and brush the tops again with eggwash, being careful not to let it
dribble down the sides as this will hinder their rise in the oven. Sprinkle
a little cheese onto each scone and bake for 15 minutes until golden
brown. Transfer to a wire rack to cool.

These biscuits can be served as a snack or with cheese at the end of a meal. Any cheeses go well with them – they're great.

Cheese Biscuits

375 g/13 oz strong white flour, plus extra for dusting

1 teaspoon salt

125 g/4 oz butter, softened

40 ml/1½ fl oz water

2 medium eggs, beaten in separate bowls

For the flavourings

2 tablespoons poppy seeds

40 g/1½ oz Gruyère cheese

2 teaspoons caraway seeds

Makes 30–40 thin biscuits

Put the flour, salt, butter, water and 1 beaten egg into a bowl and mix well for 5 minutes.

Divide the dough into three pieces, and add the poppy seeds to one, the Gruyère to the second, and the caraway seeds to the third. Wrap each piece in clingfilm and chill for 2 hours.

Preheat the oven to 220°C/425°F/mark 7. Line a baking tray. Using a rolling pin, roll out each piece of dough on a lightly floured surface to about 3 mm/⅛ inch thick. Using a round cutter of your choice (I use one 7.5 cm/3 inches wide), cut out the dough. Place the discs on the baking tray and brush with the remaining beaten egg.

Bake for 15 minutes until golden brown, then transfer onto a wire rack to cool. Serve warm or cold.

French Breads

The French are passionate about their bread – historically, the shaving of bakers' heads for selling underweight bread was not uncommon. This loaf typifies French bread – a big, bold, hearty loaf full of flavour. Serve toasted or with cheese, it's a must try!

The ubiquitous baguette, filled with cheese and ham then toasted, is my lunch any day. Serve with a glass of chilled Chablis. Start this bread the day before.

Pain de Campagne *Illustrated*

Baguette

400 g/14 oz strong white flour, plus extra for dusting

100 g/3½ oz rye flour

1 tablespoon salt

30 g/1 oz yeast

50 g/2 oz butter, softened

1 large bunch fresh oregano, destalked and chopped

300 ml/½ pint water

Makes 1 loaf

Put all the ingredients except the water into a bowl, then slowly add the water and mix in with your hands until all the flour on the sides of the bowl has been incorporated.

Tip the dough out onto a lightly floured surface and knead for 6 minutes. Put the dough back in the bowl and leave for 2 hours.

Line a baking tray. Tip the dough out onto your floured surface and shape into a ball, then slightly flatten with your hands and dust with flour. Using a knife, mark out a square shape on top of the dough, put on the baking tray and leave to rise for 1 hour.

Preheat the oven to 220°C/425°F/ mark 7. Bake for 30 minutes until golden brown, then transfer to a wire rack to cool.

500 g/1 lb 2 oz strong white flour

20 g/¾ oz yeast

warm water to mix

1 tablespoon salt

50 g/2 oz butter, softened

Makes 1 loaf

Mix 200 g/7 oz of the flour with all the yeast and enough warm water to make a thick batter, then leave to rise overnight.

Add the rest of the flour, the salt and butter to the dough and slowly add enough water to make a soft, pliable dough. Rest the dough for 1 hour.

Line a baking tray. Bang the air out of the dough and roll into a baguette shape. Put it on the baking tray and leave to prove for 1 hour.

Preheat the oven to 220°C/425°F/ mark 7. Before the dough goes into the oven, using a sharp knife, make slashes along its length. Bake for 30 minutes, then transfer to a wire rack to cool.

This is a traditional French bread, flat and leaf-shaped, very much like the focaccia of Italy. It's eaten with cheese and salads. There are many flavours that go well in this style of bread – try peppers, ham, Cheddar cheese or plain basil – c'est bon!

Onion and Bacon Fougasse

400 g/14 oz strong white flour

30 g/1 oz yeast

200 ml/7½ fl oz water

1½ teaspoons salt

75 ml/3 fl oz olive oil

1 onion, peeled, finely chopped and fried until translucent

3 rashers of back bacon, finely chopped and fried

Makes 3 loaves

Line three baking trays. Put 200 g/7 oz of the flour with all the yeast and about 175 ml/6 fl oz of water into a bowl and beat together for about 3 minutes into a thick batter. Leave to rise and fall – this should take 3–4 hours.

Add the rest of the flour and water along with the salt, 60 ml/2 fl oz of the oil, the fried onions and bacon and knead well for 5 minutes. Put back in the bowl and leave to rise for 1 hour.

Divide the dough into three pieces. Using a rolling pin, flatten each piece to about 2.5 cm/1 inch high, then shape each roughly into a circle. Using your knife, cut two diagonal slashes down the middle of each circle and three diagonal slashes on each side. Brush lightly with the remaining olive oil, place on the baking trays and leave to rise for 1 hour.

Preheat the oven to 230°C/450°F/mark 8. Bake the bread for 15 minutes until golden brown, then transfer to a wire rack to cool.

I sold this by the truckful on Saturdays from our shop in Canterbury.

Brie and Basil Bread

500 g/1 lb 2 oz wholemeal flour, plus extra for dusting

50 ml/2 fl oz olive oil

1 tablespoon salt

20 g/¾ oz yeast

water to mix

100 g/3½ oz Brie cheese, thinly sliced

a handful of freshly chopped basil leaves

Makes 1 loaf

Put the flour, olive oil and salt into a large bowl and rub the mix together. Dilute the yeast in a little warm water and add to the bowl. Slowly add water, mixing with your hand as you do, until all the flour has been incorporated and your dough feels soft to the touch.

Tip the dough out onto a lightly floured surface and knead for 6 minutes until you have a pliable dough. Put back in the bowl and leave to rise for 2 hours.

Line a baking tray. Tip the dough out onto your floured surface and, using your hands, shape into a mini baguette, then place on the baking tray. Coat the top with wholemeal flour and make several slashes in the dough lengthways down the middle. Push the Brie and basil into the grooves, then rest the dough for 2 hours.

Preheat the oven to 200°C/400°F/mark 6. Bake the bread for 20 minutes until golden brown, then transfer to a wire rack to cool.

A truly French bread. The immortal line uttered by Marie Antoinette, allegedly, 'Let them eat cake', should have read 'Let them eat brioche', as this was more likely a scenario. You need to start this the day before.

Brioche Têtes

375 g/13 oz strong white flour

40 g/1½ oz caster sugar

15 g/½ oz yeast

1 teaspoon salt

75 ml/3 fl oz milk

3 medium eggs, plus 1 egg, beaten, for eggwash

185 g/6½ oz butter, softened

8–10 paper muffin cases

Makes 8–10 brioche

Put the flour, sugar, yeast, salt, milk and the 3 eggs in a food processor and process, using the blade, for about 5 minutes to a smooth dough. If mixing by hand this will take 8 minutes.

Add the butter to the dough and mix for a further 5 minutes in the mixer or 10 minutes by hand. Put the dough into a bowl, cover and leave in the fridge overnight.

The dough should now be stiff and easily shaped. Cut the dough into 75 g/3 oz pieces and cut a quarter off each piece. Using your hands, shape the quarters and the larger pieces into balls. Put each large piece of dough into a muffin case and push a smaller dough on top of each one. Leave the brioche in a warm place to rise for 1 hour.

Preheat the oven to 200°C/400°F/mark 6. Brush the brioche with the eggwash and bake for 15 minutes until golden brown. Transfer to a wire rack to cool.

Brioche was rumoured to have been first made around the area where Brie is made, so this is a marriage made in heaven. You need to make the dough the day before.

During my time at the Dorchester Hotel in London, this brioche was a great favourite of the Sultan of Brunei. It's fabulous when toasted and served on a bed of rocket salad, with a lemon and dill vinaigrette. You need to make the dough the day before.

Brie and Brioche Parcels *Illustrated*

1 quantity Brioche dough (see page 43)

flour for dusting

250 g/9 oz Brie cheese

1 egg, beaten, for eggwash

Makes 1 brioche

Roll out the brioche dough on a lightly floured surface to about 5 mm/¼ inch thick. Place the cheese in the middle of the dough and fold the sides of the dough neatly onto the middle.

Turn the parcel over and brush the top with some of the eggwash, then place in the fridge for 1 hour.

Preheat the oven to 200°C/400°F/mark 6. Line a baking tray. Brush the parcel with eggwash again, then, using the back of a knife, score a criss-cross pattern over the parcel. Place on the baking tray and bake for 15 minutes until golden brown. Serve warm.

Salmon Brioche

500 g/1 lb 2 oz strong white flour, plus extra for dusting

1½ teaspoons salt

50 g/2 oz caster sugar

4 medium eggs

20 g/¾ oz yeast

50 ml/2 fl oz milk

250 g/9 oz butter, softened

150 g/5 oz smoked salmon, sliced

Makes 2 brioche

Put the flour into a bowl with the salt, sugar, eggs and yeast and gently rub the mixture together. Add the milk, then use your hands to mix the ingredients together for 5 minutes. Leave the dough in a warm place to rest for 30 minutes.

Slowly add the butter to the dough, kneading for a further 6 minutes, then leave the dough in the fridge overnight. The dough will solidify in the fridge.

Separate the dough into 16 pieces. Lightly cover your hands with flour and roll each piece into a small ball. Push your thumb halfway through the middle of each dough ball and place a slither of salmon inside. Reshape, using a little flour to stop the dough sticking to your hands, and repeat this process until you have 16 mini-brioche.

Lightly grease and line two 450 g/1 lb loaf tins. Place eight of the balls closely together in each tin and leave to prove until they have reached three-quarters of the way up the tins – about 1 hour.

Preheat the oven to 200°C/400°F/mark 6. Bake the brioche for 15 minutes, then turn out onto a wire rack and leave to cool slightly before serving.

Brioche is a delicate bread and, with the apricots inside, when toasted is a full breakfast in itself. You need to start this the day before.

Apricot Brioche

375 g/13 oz strong
white flour

40 g/1½ oz
caster sugar

15 g/½ oz yeast

pinch of salt

75 ml/3 fl oz milk

3 medium eggs

185 g/6½ oz
butter, softened

150 g/5 oz soft,
ready-to-eat dried
apricots, diced

Makes 3 brioche

Put the flour, sugar, yeast, salt, milk and eggs in a food mixer and process, using the blade, for about 5 minutes to a smooth dough. If mixing by hand this will take 8 minutes. Add the butter and mix for a further 5 minutes in a mixer or 10 minutes by hand. Tip the dough out into a bowl, cover and leave in the fridge overnight.

Grease three 450 g/1 lb loaf tins. The dough should now be stiff and easily shaped. Divide the dough into 75 g/3 oz pieces and add 1 teaspoon of the apricots into the middle of each piece. Fold the dough over the filling and shape into little balls. Put the balls in the tins in rows of 2 balls, 1 ball, 2 balls, and so on until the tin is full. Each tin should hold no more than 10 pieces. Leave the brioche to rise for 1–2 hours.

Preheat the oven to 200°C/400°F/mark 6. Bake the brioche for 20 minutes until golden brown, then turn out and cool on a wire rack. Cut into slices, toast and serve with lots of butter.

I've included croissants – although not essentially a bread – because they are risen with yeast and have become a symbol throughout the world for everything French. Every French pastry chef I've met has claimed he has the best recipe for croissants. I've tried and tested them all and come to the conclusion that mine are the best! Take a bite and see what you think. You need to start this the day before.

Croissant

20 g/¾ oz yeast

625 g/1 lb 7 oz strong white flour, plus extra for dusting

1½ teaspoons salt

75 g/3 oz caster sugar

water to mix

500 g/1 lb 2 oz butter, chilled

1 egg, beaten, for eggwash

Makes about 40 croissants

Dilute the yeast with a little warm water and put with the flour, salt and sugar into a large mixing bowl. Using a wooden spoon, slowly mix in a little water until the dough becomes pliable. Tip the dough out onto a lightly floured surface and knead well until it feels elastic. Put the dough back in the bowl and leave in the fridge for 1 hour.

Turn out the chilled dough onto your floured surface and roll it into a rectangle 60 x 30.5 cm/24 x 12 inches. Flatten the chilled butter into a rectangle about 1 cm/½ inch thick and lay it over two-thirds of the dough. Bring the uncovered third of the dough into the centre, then fold the covered top third down, so that your dough is now in three layers. Give the dough parcel a quarter turn so that the fold is on the right. Return the dough to the fridge to chill for 1 hour.

Scatter some more flour over your table and roll out the dough to the same-sized rectangle as before. Repeat the folding process, one side on top of the other, turn the dough again and place the dough back in the fridge for 1 hour. You will need to repeat this whole process twice more before leaving the dough to rest, wrapped in clingfilm, overnight.

Line a baking tray. Using a rolling pin, flatten the dough to 3 mm/⅛ inch thick and cut into 20.5 x 20.5 cm/8 x 8 inch squares. Cut each square diagonally, making two triangles. Lay the triangles on a lightly floured surface with the narrow points away from you, then roll each piece up from the edge nearest you towards the point, ending with the tip underneath. Bend the ends round to make the traditional croissant shape. Put the croissants on the baking tray and leave to rise for 1½ hours.

Preheat the oven to 200°C/400°F/mark 6. Brush the croissants lightly with the eggwash and bake for 10–15 minutes until golden brown, then transfer to a wire rack to cool.

On cold winter nights in the bakery I used to wait patiently for these to come out of the oven, still oozing with cheese. They're great with coffee or as a light snack.

Cheese and Ham Croissant

1 quantity Croissant
dough (see page 48)

1 egg, beaten,
for eggwash

For the filling

200 g/7 oz
honey-glazed ham

200 g/7 oz Cheddar
cheese, grated

*Makes 30–40
croissants*

Make the croissant dough as on page 48 up to the point where it is ready to shape. (At this stage you do not have to use all the dough, it can be frozen and will keep for 2–3 months. To defrost the dough, bring out of the freezer the night before and thaw overnight.)

Line several baking trays. Using a rolling pin, roll the dough out to a rectangle, 3 mm/⅛ inch thick. Cut the rectangle into 10 cm/4 inch strips, then cut each strip diagonally into triangles. Once you have the triangles for the croissant, cut replica shapes from the ham and place on the dough and top with a little grated cheese. Lay the triangles with the narrow points away from you, then roll each triangle up towards the point, ending with the tip underneath. Bend the ends round to make the traditional croissant shape. Put the croissants on the baking trays, brush with eggwash and leave to rise for 2 hours.

Preheat the oven to 200°C/400°F/mark 6. Bake the croissants for 20 minutes until golden brown, then transfer to a wire rack to cool.

If there is no other recipe in this book you try, do try this –
I promise you, it's heaven. And if you've fallen out with your partner,
make these and you'll kiss and make up in no time!

Chocolate Croissants

1 quantity of Croissant dough (see page 48)

3 Terry's Chocolate Orange eggs

1 egg, beaten, for eggwash

apricot jam, warmed, to glaze

Makes 30–40

Make the croissant dough as on page 48 up to the point where it is ready to shape.

Line several baking trays. Roll out the dough to 3 mm/⅛ inch thick and cut into 7.5 x 12.5 cm/3 x 5 inch rectangles. Put a piece of a Chocolate Orange at the short end of each rectangle and roll up into a parcel. Brush each one with eggwash, place on the baking tray and leave to rise for 2 hours.

Preheat the oven to 200°C/400°F/mark 6. Bake the croissants for 20 minutes until golden brown, then remove from the oven and brush each one with the apricot jam.

Italian Breads

This recipe is perfect for making pizzas and garlic bread: simply flatten the dough out and use as a pizza base or brush with garlic oil and you have instant garlic bread.

Ciabatta

500 g/1 lb 2 oz strong white flour, plus extra for dusting

375 ml/13 fl oz water

30 g/1 oz yeast

1 tablespoon salt

30 ml/1 fl oz olive oil

Makes 4 loaves

Put 300 g/11 oz of the flour into a bowl with 200 ml/7½ fl oz of water and the yeast. Using a hand whisk, whisk for 5 minutes then leave to ferment for 4 hours.

Add the remaining flour and water, the salt and olive oil. Whisk briskly for 5 minutes, then leave in the bowl for 2 hours.

Tip the dough out onto a lightly floured surface and divide into two pieces. Stretch each piece of dough into a 20.5 cm/8 inch loaf then allow to rest for 1 hour.

Line a baking tray. Divide each piece of dough into two. Stretch each of the four loaves back to 20.5 cm/8 inches, transfer to the baking tray and leave to rest for 1 hour.

Preheat the oven to 200°C/400°F/mark 6. Dust the loaves with flour and bake for 25–30 minutes until golden brown, then transfer to a wire rack to cool.

The idea for this pizza came from a Sicilian friend who had moved to Cyprus, opened a pizzeria and built a beehive oven to bake the pizzas in. The secret of a good pizza is to use fresh ingredients and to keep the flavours simple – you want to be able to taste the ciabatta base and not have it overwhelmed by the toppings.

Ham and Cream Pizza

For the tomato sauce

2 tablespoons olive oil

1 small onion, peeled and finely chopped

1 garlic clove, peeled and chopped

1 tablespoon tomato purée

400 g can chopped tomatoes

2 tablespoons freshly chopped basil

2 bay leaves

1 teaspoon caster sugar

salt and freshly ground black pepper

For the dough

1 quantity pizza (Ciabatta) dough (see page 54)

flour for dusting

60 g/2½ oz Gorgonzola blue cheese, crumbled

150 g/5 oz mozzarella cheese, crumbled

250 g/9 oz mature Cheddar cheese, crumbled

1 small carton double cream

8 thin slices of Virginia ham

Makes 1 pizza

To make the sauce, heat the oil in a pan and sauté the onion until translucent, then add the garlic and fry gently for a further minute. Stir in the rest of the ingredients and season to taste. Bring the sauce to the boil, then leave to simmer for about 30 minutes. Before using, remove the bay leaves.

Meanwhile, preheat the oven to 230°C/450°F/mark 8. Roll out the dough on a lightly floured surface to a 25.5 cm/10 inch diameter circle and place on a baking tray. Bake for 5 minutes (this kills the yeast in the dough).

Lightly spread the tomato sauce onto your pizza base and sprinkle sparingly with the Gorgonzola, then cover with the mozzarella and Cheddar cheeses. Pour the double cream all over the pizza and bake for 20–25 minutes until golden brown.

Take the pizza out of the oven and place thin layers of ham on the top. Serve immediately.

Bruschetta is great party food and you can make it just a couple of hours before your guests arrive. It also makes a good snack.

Tomato Bruschetta

450 g/1 lb ripe tomatoes, peeled and cut into small pieces

3 tablespoons olive oil

10 basil leaves, torn in pieces

salt and freshly ground black pepper to taste

10–15 Ciabatta slices (see page 54)

2 cloves of garlic, peeled and halved

Serves 4

Put the tomatoes in the oil with the basil leaves, season to taste and leave to marinate.

Toast the Ciabatta, then rub each side with the garlic. Spoon some of the tomato mixture onto each slice and serve warm.

Olive Bruschetta

200 g/7 oz black olives, pitted

juice of 1 lemon

1 tablespoon olive oil

salt and freshly ground black pepper to taste

10–15 ciabatta slices (see page 54)

2 cloves of garlic, peeled and halved

Serves 4

Put the olives, lemon juice and oil in a mixer and whiz for 2 minutes until you have a smooth paste. Season to taste.

Toast the ciabatta, then rub each side with the garlic. Cover each slice with the olive mixture and serve warm.

The aromas in your kitchen when making this are unbelievable. If you're trying to sell your house make this an hour before the potential buyers view it. A sale is guaranteed.

Basil and Olive Focaccia

500 g/1 lb 2 oz strong white flour, plus extra for dusting

1 tablespoon salt

100 ml/3½ fl oz olive oil

30 g/1 oz yeast

300 ml/½ pint water

125 g/4 oz black olives, pitted but left whole

handful freshly chopped basil leaves

salt water made with 30 g/1 oz salt dissolved in 100 ml/3½ fl oz warm water

Makes 1 loaf

Put the flour, salt, half the olive oil, the yeast and water into a large bowl and mix with your hand for 3 minutes until all the flour has been picked up.

Tip the dough out onto a lightly floured surface and knead well for 6 minutes. The dough should be quite sticky. Put the dough back in the bowl and leave at room temperature for 2 hours.

Line a baking tray. Mix 100 g/3½ oz of the olives and all the basil into the dough, then flatten the dough out onto the baking tray to about 2.5 cm/1 inch thick. Brush the top of the dough with a little olive oil and make indentations in the top with your fingers. Leave to rise for 1 hour.

Preheat the oven to 230°C/450°F/mark 8. Brush the top of the dough with the salt water and drizzle with the remaining olive oil, then stud the remaining olives on top of the dough.

Bake for 25 minutes until golden brown, then transfer to a wire rack to cool a little. Serve warm with an olive salad.

This is based on a bread I made while working in Italy in 2002.
You do not need the sun belting down – but it helps!

Focaccia Pugliese with Mozzarella

500 g/1 lb 2 oz strong
white flour, plus extra
for dusting

1 tablespoon salt

30 g/1 oz yeast

100 ml/3½ fl oz
olive oil

300 ml/½ pint water

salt water made from
30 g/1 oz salt
dissolved in
100 ml/3½ fl oz
warm water

2 packets buffalo
mozzarella, drained
and crumbled

*Makes 2 small or
1 large bread*

Put the flour, salt, yeast, half the olive oil and all the water into a bowl and mix together to make a pliable dough. Tip the dough out onto a lightly floured surface and knead for 5 minutes. Put the dough back in the bowl and leave to rest for 1 hour.

Line a baking tray. Divide the dough into two pieces, or leave as 1 large bread. Stretch the dough out with your hands so it is about 5 cm/ 2 inches thick and oval in shape. Put it on the baking tray and prick the top with a knife (this will restrict its growth). Brush the top with about 30 ml/1 fl oz of the salt water and the remaining olive oil. Cover the top of the bread with the mozzarella, then leave the dough to rise for 45 minutes.

Preheat the oven to 220°C/425°F/mark 7. Bake the bread for 30 minutes, then transfer to a wire rack to cool. Serve with an olive salad and a glass of good Tuscan wine like Montelpulciano.

Focaccia are both gorgeous to look at and to eat. They epitomize the Italian philosophy on bread – simple but effective flavourings. You will need to prepare the garlic oil the night before.

Focaccia Pugliese with Tomatoes and Garlic

4 garlic cloves, peeled and crushed

150 ml/¼ pint olive oil

500 g/1 lb 2 oz strong white flour, plus extra for dusting

1 tablespoon salt

20 g/¾ oz yeast

300 ml/½ pint water

salt water made from 30 g/1 oz salt dissolved in 100 ml/3½ fl oz warm water

6 plum tomatoes, thinly sliced

Makes 1 loaf

Add the garlic to the olive oil then leave to infuse overnight.

Put the flour, salt, yeast, half the infused olive oil and all the water into a large bowl and mix together for 4 minutes. Tip out onto a lightly floured surface and knead for 6 minutes, then put back in the bowl to rest for 1 hour.

Line a baking tray. Tip the dough out onto your floured surface and roll out a rectangle about 2.5 cm/1 inch thick. Sprinkle with the salt water and the remaining olive oil, then, using a knife, prick the top of the dough all over. Place the tomatoes on top of the dough, then put on the baking tray and leave to rise for 1 hour.

Preheat the oven to 220°C/425°F/mark 7. Bake the bread for 25–30 minutes until golden brown. Eat warm.

I made this with a couple of Sicilian friends when I was in Italy, and was astounded by the flavours from the potatoes – they marry so well with the rosemary and bread.

Potato Focaccia Pugliese

500 g/1 lb 2 oz strong white flour, plus extra for dusting

1 tablespoon salt

20 g/¾ oz yeast

300 ml/½ pint water

olive oil

8–10 new potatoes, scrubbed and thinly sliced

rock salt, to sprinkle

2 sprigs fresh rosemary, destalked

Makes 1 loaf

Put the flour, salt, yeast and water into a bowl and mix to form a dough. Leave in the bowl to double in size for about 1 hour.

Line a baking tray. Tip the dough out of the bowl onto the baking tray and flatten with your hands, then brush with olive oil and, using your fingers, make indentations over the surface. Layer the potatoes over the top, sprinkle with a little rock salt and stud with the rosemary sprigs. Leave to rise on the baking tray for 1 hour.

Preheat the oven to 230°C/450°F/mark 8. Bake the bread for 30 minutes. Remove from the oven and brush the loaf with more olive oil, then transfer to a wire rack and serve when cooled.

This focaccia perfectly complements tomato-based pasta dishes and thick winter soups. For extra richness drizzle over a little olive oil and sprinkle with chopped garlic.

Mushroom, Onion and Basil Focaccia

500 g/1 lb 2 oz strong white flour

1½ teaspoons salt

15 g/½ oz yeast

60 ml/2 fl oz olive oil, plus extra for frying and drizzling

water to mix

100 g/3½ oz button mushrooms, chopped

3 onions, peeled and chopped

butter for frying

freshly chopped basil leaves

rock salt, for sprinkling

Makes 1 loaf

Put the flour, salt and yeast into a bowl and mix thoroughly by hand. Add the olive oil, then slowly add sufficient water to make a dough. Mix until the dough comes away from the sides of the bowl. Tip the dough out onto a lightly floured surface and knead well for 5 minutes. When the dough is pliable, put back in the bowl, cover and leave to rest for about 1 hour.

Meanwhile, fry the mushrooms and onions in a little butter and olive oil until browned. Set aside.

Add the mushrooms, onions and a handful of chopped basil to the dough, pressing them into the mixture with your hands.

Grease a 30.5 cm/12 inch loaf tin. Transfer the dough to the tin and press out evenly to the edges. Leave to rest for 30 minutes.

Using your fingers, make indentations all over the dough, brush lightly with olive oil and sprinkle with rock salt. Leave to prove for 1½ hours.

Preheat the oven to 200°C/400°F/mark 6. Bake the bread for 20–30 minutes until golden brown. Eat warm.

You can try sunblushed tomatoes in this recipe – they work just as well. The aromas in your kitchen while you are making this bread will tempt not just you, but your neighbours, too.

Olive and Sun-dried Tomato Bread

500 g/1 lb 2 oz strong white flour, plus extra for dusting

1½ teaspoons salt

40 ml/1½ fl oz olive oil

20 g/¾ oz yeast

300 ml/½ pint warm water

150 g/5 oz black Greek olives, pitted

100 g/3½ oz sun-dried tomatoes, chopped

Makes 2 loaves

Put the flour in a large bowl and add the salt, olive oil and yeast. Slowly add the warm water, folding it in with your hand until the dough becomes pliable.

Tip the dough out onto a lightly floured surface and knead for 5 minutes, then return the dough to the bowl, cover and leave for 1 hour in a warm place.

Line a baking tray. Divide the dough into two and add half the olives and tomatoes to each piece and work in well. Mould into a round shape and press firmly down to flatten. Sprinkle flour over each dough and mark a cross in each. Put on the baking tray and leave to prove for 1 hour in a warm place.

Preheat the oven to 220°C/425°F/mark 7. Bake the breads for about 30 minutes until golden brown, then transfer to a wire rack to cool.

This is an Italian-inspired bread from Tuscany. Their tomatoes are so juicy and full of flavour that it was a natural thing to try them out in one of my breads.

Try drying the tomatoes yourself in an oven – cut them in slices, sprinkle with olive oil and leave in a low oven – 110°C/225°F/mark ¼ – overnight.

Tomato and Basil Bread

500 g/1 lb 2 oz strong white flour, plus extra for dusting

1 tablespoon salt

30 g/1 oz yeast

60 ml/2 fl oz olive oil

300 ml/½ pint water

100 g/3½ oz sunblushed tomatoes

2 packets fresh basil, roughly chopped

Makes 1 loaf

Put the flour, salt, yeast, oil and water into a bowl and mix gently by hand to bring them together. When all the flour has been incorporated, tip the dough out onto a lightly floured surface and knead for 5 minutes. When the dough is pliable, transfer it to a bowl, cover and leave to rest for about 1 hour.

Line a baking tray. Add the tomatoes and basil to the dough and work in well. Shape the dough into a long sausage and tie in a knot. Place on the tray and leave to rise for 1 hour.

Preheat the oven to 230°C/450°F/mark 8. Bake the loaf for 30 minutes until golden brown, then transfer to a wire rack to cool.

You need to start this the day before.

I spent the summer of 2002 in and around Tuscany making bread with local bakers. This bread brings back good memories. The lack of salt in the recipe will be compensated for by the fermentation of the dough. You need to start this the day before.

Pane Tuscana

Pane Tuscana with Dolcelatte Cheese

500 g/1 lb 2 oz Italian tipo 00 flour, plus extra for dusting

15 g/½ oz yeast

250 ml/8½ fl oz water

60 ml/2 fl oz olive oil

Makes 1 loaf

Put half the flour, all the yeast and 150 ml/¼ pint of the water into a bowl and mix until you have a thick batter consistency. Leave to rise for 9 hours or overnight.

Mix in the remaining flour and water and the olive oil and knead for 5 minutes. Leave in the bowl to rise for 1 hour.

Line a baking tray. Tip the dough out onto a lightly floured surface and shape into a ball. Rub flour all over the ball so it is covered, then make several slashes randomly all over the loaf. Leave to rise on the baking tray for 1 hour.

Preheat the oven to 220°C/425°F/mark 7. Bake the loaf for 30 minutes, then leave to cool slightly and serve warm.

500 g/1 lb 2 oz Italian tipo 00 flour, plus extra for dusting

15 g/½ oz yeast

250 ml/8½ fl oz water

60 ml/2 fl oz olive oil

150 g/5 oz Dolcelatte cheese

Makes 1 loaf

Mix half the flour with all the yeast and 150 ml/¼ pint of the water until you have a thick batter-like consistency. Leave to rise for 9 hours.

Line a baking tray. Add the remaining flour and water and the olive oil to the dough and mix in well, then knead for 5 minutes. Slowly add the cheese – it will get very messy but persevere, add a little flour if it gets too wet. Roll up into a sausage and join the ends together. Dust with flour, put on the baking tray and leave to rise for 1 hour.

Preheat the oven to 220°C/425°F/mark 7. Bake the bread for 30 minutes, allow to cool a little and serve warm.

These make great snack food; my son Joshua loves them. They can be frozen in dough form and thawed in about 3 hours.

This is a recipe that is used in several well-known hotels. The straws are very quick to make and when the pastry is baked it doubles in size and is a real mouthful.

Grissini Sticks

250 g/9 oz strong white flour, plus extra for dusting

pinch of salt

5 g/¼ oz yeast

1 large tablespoon olive oil

150 ml/¼ pint water

sesame or poppy seeds

Makes about 30 sticks

Put the flour, salt, yeast and olive oil into a bowl and mix together. Gradually add the water (you probably won't need all of it) and mix until all the flour has been incorporated from the sides of the bowl. Tip the dough out onto a lightly floured surface and knead for 5 minutes. Return the dough to the bowl and leave to rest for 30 minutes.

Preheat the oven to 220°C/425°F/mark 7. Line a baking tray. Rip the dough into hand-sized pieces and roll each out into thin strips about 25.5 cm/10 inches in length. Moisten your hands a little and roll each strip in sesame or poppy seeds, then place on the baking tray. Bake for 20 minutes until golden brown.

Cheese Straws

1 packet ready-made puff pastry

flour for dusting

1 egg, beaten

30 g/1 oz paprika

200 g/7 oz Parmesan cheese, finely grated

Makes 30–40 sticks

Roll out the puff pastry on a lightly floured surface to about 1 cm/½ inch thick and brush with beaten egg. Sprinkle with paprika and coat generously with the Parmesan.

Fold one third in and then fold the remaining dough on top and rest the pastry in the fridge for 30 minutes. Repeat this twice more.

Preheat the oven to 200°C/400°F/mark 6. Line a baking tray. Roll out the dough to 1 cm/½ inch thick and cut into long strips. Twist each strip in opposite directions to create a spiral effect, then place on the baking tray and bake for 15 minutes. Serve warm.

Traditional Breads

Authentic naan needs to be baked in a specially made brick oven, but I decided to shallow-fry the dough instead, which gives it this light and fluffy, golden finish. It's excellent as finger food, cut into thin slices and served with a chilled aubergine and crème fraîche dip.

I was asked by a chef to come up with a naan to go with his extensive buffet. I love curries so this was the obvious recipe.

Naan Bread

Curried Naan Bread *Illustrated*

500 g/1 lb 2 oz strong white flour, plus extra for dusting

1½ teaspoons salt

15 g/½ oz yeast

water to mix

1 teaspoon cumin seeds

1 teaspoon caraway seeds

olive oil for frying

Makes 3 naan

Line a baking tray. Put the flour, salt and yeast into a bowl and add enough water to make a soft, but not sloppy dough. Add the seeds, then divide the dough into three pieces, put on the baking tray and leave to rest for 1 hour.

Turn the dough out onto a lightly floured surface and, using a rolling pin, flatten each piece into a circle, 25.5 cm/ 10 inches in diameter, and leave to rest for 5 minutes.

Heat a frying pan to a medium heat and add a splash of olive oil. Shallow-fry each naan until browned on both sides, then set aside to cool slightly before serving.

500 g/1 lb 2 oz strong white flour, plus extra for dusting

1½ teaspoons salt

1 tablespoon olive oil, plus extra for frying

50 g/2 oz mild curry powder

15 g/½ oz yeast

300 ml/½ pint water

100 g/3½ oz sultanas

3 tablespoons mango chutney

Makes 6 naan

Put the flour, salt, oil, curry powder, yeast and water into a bowl and mix together for 2 minutes. Tip out onto a lightly floured surface and knead for 5 minutes until the dough is soft and pliable. Leave to rise for 30 minutes.

Line a baking tray. Incorporate the sultanas and chutney into the dough. Divide the dough into six pieces, put on the baking tray and leave to rest for 1 hour.

Turn the dough out onto a lightly floured surface and, using a rolling pin, flatten each piece into a circle, 25.5 cm/ 10 inches in diameter, put back on the tray and leave to rest for 5 minutes.

Heat a frying pan to a medium heat and add a splash of olive oil. Shallow-fry each dough until browned on both sides, then set aside to cool slightly before serving.

Paratha is a very moist, chewy bread – great for dunking in your curry. It can be fried in a frying pan.

Paratha

400 g/14 oz wholemeal flour, plus extra for dusting

3 tablespoons vegetable oil, plus extra for frying

salt

600 ml/1 pint water

For the filling

1 tablespoon vegetable oil

⅓ teaspoon cumin seeds

3 green chillies, deseeded and finely chopped

1 teaspoon ground coriander

30 g/1 oz sultanas

Makes 4–6

Put the flour, oil and salt into a large bowl and slowly mix in the water until a dough is formed. Knead until smooth, then cover the dough with a clean cloth and leave for 20 minutes.

Meanwhile, make the filling. Heat the oil in a frying pan and add the cumin seeds and chillies. Fry, stirring, for 1 minute, then add the coriander and sultanas and mix well. Cook gently, stirring now and then, for 5 minutes, then put to one side.

Divide the dough into small balls and lightly coat each ball with flour. Roll each ball out on a lightly floured surface to form thin, flat breads, or parathas, about 5–10 cm/2–4 inches across.

Heat a griddle pan until hot. Brush a paratha with a little oil and place on the griddle. Add 2–3 tablespoons of the filling into the middle of the paratha and fold over to enclose. Once the paratha has cooked underneath, turn it over and cook the other side until golden brown.

Repeat the process with the remaining parathas. Serve warm.

This recipe haunted me for many a year while I was living in Cyprus – making 500 of these a day was not my idea of fun. But this is a great recipe, given to me by George Demitriades, ex-pastry chef at the Annabelle Hotel, Paphos.

The breads make a great pre-dinner nibble, served with drinks, or they can be eaten with cheese at the end of the meal.

Lavroche

250 g/9 oz strong white flour, plus extra for dusting

100 g/3½ oz semolina

1½ teaspoons salt

1 tablespoon olive oil

100 ml/3½ fl oz water

50 ml/2 fl oz milk

1 egg, beaten, for eggwash

100 g/3½ oz sesame seeds

Fills 3 baking trays

Put all the ingredients except the eggwash and sesame seeds into a bowl and mix well, then, using your hands, knead for 5 minutes until you have a pliable dough.

Preheat the oven to 220°C/425°F/mark 7. Line a baking tray. Tip the dough out onto a lightly floured surface and, using a rolling pin, roll out until it is wafer thin – about 2–3 mm/⅛ inch thick. Use plenty of flour, but brush it off afterwards.

Cut the dough into random shapes, place on three baking trays, brush each one with eggwash and coat the top with sesame seeds. Bake for 20–30 minutes until dark brown, then serve immediately.

This recipe comes from a tiny village called Kouklia, in the south of Cyprus. Breadmaking is a social occasion for Cypriots and I spent one marvellous afternoon with friends making bread for the whole village. Afterwards we sat and ate the warm loaves with hummus, tzatziki, grilled meats and salad – fantastic!

Cypriot Olive and Coriander Bread

500 g/1 lb 2 oz strong white flour, plus extra for dusting

1½ teaspoons salt

30 ml/1 fl oz olive oil

30 g/1 oz yeast

300 ml/½ pint warm water

150 g/5 oz black Greek olives, pitted and chopped

75 g/3 oz onion, peeled and chopped

handful of fresh coriander leaves, chopped

Makes 2 loaves

Put the flour into a large bowl and add the salt and oil. Dilute the yeast in a little warm water and add to the mixture. Slowly add the warm water, folding it in with your hand until the dough becomes pliable.

Tip the dough out onto a lightly floured surface and knead for 5 minutes, then put the dough back in the bowl, cover and leave for 1 hour in a warm place.

Line a baking tray. Divide the dough into two pieces and divide half the olives, onions and coriander between each piece. The dough will now be bulging. Mould each dough into a round shape and press firmly down. Sprinkle each lightly with flour and mark a cross in each one, then put them on the baking tray and leave in a warm place for 1 hour.

Preheat the oven to 220°C/425°F/mark 7. Bake the loaves for 30 minutes until golden brown, then transfer to a wire rack to cool.

When I lived in Cyprus, every Sunday I would visit the villages of my friends and invariably make bread. This bread is very common in Cyprus and is best served with dips and a good olive salad. mastika and mechlebe are spices and seeds used in many Greek/Cypriot dishes. They have a similar flavour to fennel or aniseed, which you can use to replace them. However, most good health food shops will stock them.

Koulouri - Cypriot Village Bread

pinch of mastika

pinch of mechlebe

500 g/1 lb 2 oz strong white flour, plus extra for dusting

1½ teaspoons salt

30 g/1 oz yeast

50 ml/2 fl oz olive oil

300 ml/½ pint water

100 g/3½ oz sesame seeds

1 tablespoon black cumin seeds

1 tablespoon caraway seeds

Makes 1 loaf

Grind the mastika and mechlebe with a pestle and mortar to a smooth powder. Put the flour, salt, yeast, olive oil and water in a large bowl and blend together. Add the mastika and mechlebe powder and knead for 5 minutes, then leave the dough in the bowl to rest for 1 hour.

Tip the seeds into a large bowl and pour a little warm water on them just to dampen them. This will also balloon the sesame seeds and release their juice.

Line a baking tray. Tip the dough out onto a lightly floured surface and shape into a ball. Drop the dough into the dampened seeds and turn until covered in the seeds, then place the dough on the baking tray and leave to rise for 1 hour.

Preheat the oven to 220°C/425°F/mark 7. Using a knife, make a cut around the middle of the ball and two on top. Bake in the oven for 30 minutes until golden brown, then transfer to a wire rack to cool.

This is a traditional Cypriot bread, and is eaten throughout the year in Cyprus.

Halloumi and Mint Bread

500 g/1 lb 2 oz strong white flour, plus extra for dusting

1 tablespoon salt

60 ml/2 fl oz olive oil

30 g/1 oz yeast

300 ml/½ pint water

2 packets halloumi cheese, crumbled

20 g/¾ oz dried mint

Makes 1 loaf

Put the flour, salt, olive oil and yeast into a bowl and slowly add enough water just to bring the ingredients together. Mix for 3 minutes, then tip out onto a lightly floured surface and knead for 5 minutes. (If you are using a food mixer, use the hook and mix for 5 minutes in total.) Put the dough back in the bowl and leave to rise for 1 hour.

Line a baking tray. Add the cheese and dried mint to the dough and shape into a sausage. Taper the ends and place on the baking tray to rest for 1 hour.

Preheat the oven to 220°C/425°F/mark 7. Cut diagonal slashes across the top of the dough and dust with flour. Bake for 25–30 minutes until golden brown, then transfer to a wire rack to cool.

A traditional bread made in Cyprus around Green Monday, the day the fasting starts before Easter. The bread is usually eaten with fresh vegetables and fruit.

Try using ground fennel if mastika is difficult to get hold of, but any good health food shop should stock it.

Laganes Bread

1 teaspoon mastika

500 g/1 lb 2 oz strong white flour, plus extra for dusting

1 tablespoon salt

30 g/1 oz yeast

60 ml/2 fl oz olive oil

300 ml/½ pint water

100 g/3½ oz sesame seeds

1 tablespoon caraway seeds

1½ tablespoons black cumin seeds

Makes 2 loaves

Grind the mastika with a mortar and pestle to a smooth powder. Put the flour, salt, yeast, olive oil and water into a bowl and mix together for 3 minutes. Add the mastika powder to the dough, then tip the dough out onto a lightly floured surface. Using your fingers and the heel of your palm, knead for 5 minutes, then put the dough back in the bowl and leave to rise for 1 hour.

Meanwhile, put the sesame, caraway and black cumin seeds into a bowl and pour over just enough warm water to cover. Leave for 20 minutes – this balloons the seeds and releases their flavours.

Line a baking tray. Tip the dough out onto your floured surface and divide into two pieces. Flatten each piece into an oval shape, 2.5–5 cm/1–2 inches thick, and turn them in the seed mixture until the dough is completely covered, top and bottom. Put onto the baking tray and leave to rise for 1 hour.

Preheat the oven to 220°C/425°F/mark 7. Using your finger, press holes over the top of the dough, then bake the loaves for 25 minutes until golden brown. Transfer to a wire rack to cool.

I have kept this bread as authentic as possible. You will find the mastika and mechlebe in any good health shop, but you can use ground fennel as an alternative. I've made this bread several times on television and it remains a firm favourite.

Tsoureki – Cypriot Easter Bread

500 g/1 lb 2 oz strong white flour, plus extra for dusting

60 g/2½ oz butter, softened

75 g/3 oz caster sugar

pinch of cinnamon

pinch of mastika

pinch of mechlebe

handful of sultanas

150 ml/5 fl oz milk

zest of 1 orange

1 tablespoon salt

15 g/½ oz yeast

150 ml/5 fl oz warm water

3 eggs, hardboiled in their shells with red food colouring

1 egg, beaten, for eggwash

Makes 1 loaf

Put the flour into a large bowl, add all the other ingredients except the yeast, water and eggs and mix together briefly. Dilute the yeast in a little warm water and add to the mixture. Slowly add the remaining warm water, mixing it in as you do, until you have a soft dough consistency.

Tip the dough out onto a lightly floured surface and knead until you have a pliable dough. Put the dough back in the bowl and leave to rest for 1 hour.

Line a baking tray. Divide the dough into two and roll into strips. Plait the strips together, put on the baking tray and leave to rise in a warm place for 1 hour.

Preheat the oven to 200°C/400°F/mark 6. Brush the top of the bread with eggwash and place the coloured eggs along the top of the bread. Bake for 25 minutes, then transfer to a wire rack to cool.

A traditional bread made in Eastern Europe and shaped like the
Russian Orthodox church. It makes a great afternoon treat.

Kulich

500 g/1 lb 2 oz strong
white flour, plus extra
for dusting

1½ teaspoons salt

75 g/3 oz caster sugar

75 g/3 oz butter,
softened

60 g/1 oz fresh yeast

vanilla essence

zest of 2 oranges

zest of 2 lemons

2 medium eggs

300 ml/½ pint milk

100 g/3½ oz sultanas

75 g/3 oz flaked
almonds

lemon zest, icing
sugar and water,
for topping

Makes 2 loaves

Put the flour, salt, sugar, butter, yeast, a dash of vanilla essence, the
orange and lemon zests and eggs into a bowl and blend with a little
milk just to bring the ingredients together. Slowly add the rest of the
milk, mixing with your hands, until you have a soft dough.

Tip the dough out onto a lightly floured surface and knead for a few
minutes. Put the dough back in the bowl and leave to rise for 1 hour.

Line two clean flowerpots or tins with silicone paper. Incorporate the
sultanas and almonds into the dough, then divide the dough into two
and shape each piece so that it fits into the flowerpots or tins. Leave to
rise for 1 hour.

Preheat the oven to 200°C/400°F/mark 6. Bake the flowerpots or tins in
the oven for 25–30 minutes until golden brown, then turn out onto a
wire rack to cool.

When cooled, top with a water icing made from lemon zest, icing sugar
and water.

This recipe was given to me by Sylvia Woolf when I appeared on the *This Morning* show. It has a great texture and flavour.

A traditional Arabic bread that has been made for over 3,000 years. Originally it was made with a sour culture in place of yeast and baked on olive domes set over fires.

Pesach (Passover) Bread

Pitta Bread

250 g/9 oz medium matzo meal

1 teaspoon salt

1 teaspoon caster sugar

240 ml/8 fl oz water

120 ml/4 fl oz oil

4 medium eggs

Makes 1 loaf

Put the matzo meal, salt and sugar into a bowl and mix well.

Put the water and oil in a large saucepan and bring to the boil. Add the meal mixture and stir until the dough comes away from the sides.

Add the eggs, one at a time, and stir until the mixture is smooth and thick. Leave to cool.

Line a baking tray. Flatten the dough out onto the tray and prick all over with a knife. Leave it to rest for 30 minutes.

Preheat the oven to 190°C/375°F/ mark 5. Bake the bread for about 30 minutes until browned.

500 g/1 lb 2 oz strong white flour, plus extra for dusting

1 tablespoon salt

50 g/2 oz caster sugar

50 ml/2 fl oz olive oil

30 g/1 oz yeast

300 ml/½ pint water

Makes about 7

Put all the ingredients into a bowl and mix with your hands to bind together. When a dough has formed tip out onto a lightly floured surface and knead for 5 minutes. Put back in the bowl and rest the dough for 1 hour.

Preheat the oven to 240°C/475°F/ mark 9 and put a lined baking tray inside to heat up. Tip the dough out onto the table and divide into 100 g/ 3½ oz pieces. Using a rolling pin, roll out the dough to about 1 cm/½ inch thickness. Leave to rest on the table for 5 minutes, then place on the hot baking tray in the oven and bake for 5–10 minutes. The bread will balloon up, but when you bring them out of the oven they will collapse, forming the characteristic pockets of air.

The ancient Egyptians used to bake their bread in cone-shaped terracotta pots and this is the updated version, although the herbs and onions are authentic ingredients. This bread is particularly good for dinner parties – the little pots are very eye-catching and you could even try painting them for extra effect.

Pepper and Onion Flowerpot Bread

1½ teaspoons salt

50 g/2 oz butter, softened

500 g/1 lb 2 oz strong white flour

20 g/¾ oz yeast

warm water to mix

2 large onions, peeled and finely chopped

olive oil for frying

30 g/1 oz fresh basil leaves, roughly chopped

3 red peppers, deseeded and finely chopped

Makes 3 loaves

You will need three flowerpots for this recipe, each 10 cm/4 inches in diameter and 25.5 cm/10 inches high.

Add the salt and butter to the flour and rub together. Dilute the yeast in a little water and add this to the flour, then mix in enough warm water to make the dough pliable. Knead the dough well for 5 minutes, until elasticated. Place in a bowl, cover and leave in a warm place to rest for 1 hour.

Fry the onions in a little olive oil until translucent, then set aside to cool. When cool, mix with the basil and peppers, add to the dough and blend together. Divide the dough into three equal pieces and mould them into rounds.

Line the insides and bottoms of the flowerpots with silicone paper. Place a ball of dough inside each pot and leave to prove for 1 hour.

Preheat the oven to 200°C/400°F/mark 6. Bake the flowerpots for 30 minutes. Turn the breads out onto a wire rack to cool, then return them to the unlined flowerpots for display on your dining table.

Herb and Seed Breads

This is an aromatic bread, full of flavour. Basil is a favourite herb of mine, and mixed with the coriander it's perfect. This bread is great as the base for cheese on toast.

Herb Bread

500 g/1 lb 2 oz strong white flour, plus extra for dusting

1 tablespoon salt

30 g/1 oz yeast

75 ml/3 fl oz olive oil

300 ml/½ pint water

1 packet fresh basil

1 packet fresh coriander

1 packet fresh dill

Makes 2 loaves

Put the flour, salt, yeast, olive oil and water into a bowl and, using your hands, mix together for 3 minutes. When the dough has formed, tip out onto a lightly floured surface and, using your fingers and heel of your palm, knead for 6 minutes. Put the dough back in the bowl and leave to rise for 1 hour.

Preheat the oven to 220°C/425°F/mark 7. Line a baking tray. Destalk all the herbs, then rip them up roughly and mix into the dough. Divide the dough into two pieces and shape each into a ball. Flatten slightly with your hands and cut two slashes across the top of each one. Place on the baking tray and bake for 30 minutes. Transfer to a wire rack to cool.

You can also try making this recipe with Philadelphia cream cheese instead of the ricotta, for a creamy bread with tight airholes. Either way served toasted with cheese it is unbeatable.

Ricotta and Chive Loaf

500 g/1 lb 2 oz strong white flour, plus extra for sprinkling

1½ teaspoons salt

30 g/1 oz yeast

75 ml/3 fl oz olive oil

300 ml/½ pint water

125 g/4 oz ricotta cheese

2 tablespoons snipped chives

Makes 1 loaf

Put the flour, salt, yeast, olive oil, water and cheese into a large bowl and mix with your hands for 3 minutes. Tip out onto a lightly floured surface and knead for 2 minutes, then add the chives and knead for 3 minutes more. Put the dough back in the bowl and leave to rest for 1 hour.

Line a baking tray. Tip the dough out onto a lightly floured surface and shape into a sausage shape, tapered at each end. Place the bread on the baking tray and leave to rise for 1 hour.

Preheat the oven to 220°C/425°F/mark 7. Bake the bread for 25 minutes, then transfer to a wire rack to cool.

This bread is definitely a meal on its own – serve it as a sandwich, sliced thinly, filled with roast garlic lamb and salad leaves with a lemon dressing. It also makes a great accompaniment to a thick soup topped with cheese. You need to start this bread the day before.

Potato and Dill Bread

20 g/¾ oz yeast

water to mix

500 g/1 lb 2 oz strong white flour

1½ teaspoons salt

8 medium new potatoes, scrubbed

1 garlic clove, peeled and chopped

butter and olive oil, for frying

30 g/1 oz fresh dill, destalked and chopped

Makes 2 loaves

Dilute the yeast in a little warm water. Put the flour and salt into a bowl, and add the diluted yeast. Slowly add enough water to the flour until you have a malleable dough, then leave to rest overnight.

Boil the potatoes for 5 minutes, leave to cool, then cut into quarters. Fry the potatoes and garlic in a little butter and oil until golden brown, then leave them to cool.

Grease a baking tray. Divide your dough into two pieces and flatten them into an oval shape. Place on the baking tray and leave to rise for 1–2 hours.

Preheat the oven to 230°C/450°F/mark 8. Cover the two pieces of dough equally with the potato mixture, pressing it in firmly. Sprinkle some dill over the top and bake in the oven for 25–30 minutes until golden brown. Transfer to a wire rack to cool.

A German-based rye bread, full of seeds. If this was a wine it would
be a full-bodied red.

Cereal Rye

**350 g/12 oz
dark rye flour**

**150 g/5 oz strong
white flour, plus extra
for dusting**

1½ teaspoons salt

30 g/1 oz yeast

**75 ml/3 fl oz
malt extract**

300 ml/½ pint water

**2 teaspoons caraway
seeds**

**75 g/3 oz sunflower
seeds**

**75 g/3 oz
sesame seeds**

**1 tablespoon
poppy seeds**

*Makes 2 x 450 g/
1 lb loaves*

Put all the ingredients into a bowl and mix well. Knead gently for
5 minutes to bring together, then tip out onto a lightly floured surface
and knead with your fingers and palms for 6 minutes. Put the dough
back in the bowl and leave to rest for 2 hours.

Grease two 450 g/1 lb loaf tins. Divide the dough into two pieces and
form each into a sausage shape. Put into the tins and leave to rise for
1 hour.

Preheat the oven to 220°C/425°F/mark 7. Bake the loaves for
30 minutes, then turn out onto a wire rack to cool.

These breads have been spotted in bakeries around the Middle East,
Greece and in the tombs of the Pharoahs.
The rings can be cut open and filled with cheese and onion, to make
a great snack.

Sesame Rings

**500 g/1 lb 2 oz
strong white flour,
plus extra for dusting**

1½ teaspoons salt

30 g/1 oz yeast

30 ml/1 fl oz olive oil

300 ml/½ pint water

sesame seeds, to coat

Makes 10–15

Put all the ingredients except the sesame seeds into a bowl and roughly
mix together. When the dough has formed, tip it onto a lightly floured
surface and knead for 5 minutes. Put the dough back into the bowl and
leave to double in size.

Line two baking trays. Divide the dough into 75 g/3 oz pieces and roll
them out to about 10 cm/4 inch-long sausage shapes, then join the
ends to form a ring. When all the rings have been made roll them in
the sesame seeds, place them on the baking trays and leave to rise
for 1 hour.

Preheat the oven to 220°C/425°F/mark 7. Bake the rings for
25 minutes until golden brown, then transfer to a wire rack to cool.

I was asked to make a bread for Spyros, a friend in Cyprus; he loved sunflower seeds so I came up with this. I hope you like it. It will last longer if the butter is omitted, but it gives it a richer flavour.

This loaf you love or you hate, mainly because of the caraway seeds. You need to start this the night before.

Sunflower Seed Bread *Illustrated*

250 g/9 oz wholemeal flour	Put the flours, salt, yeast, butter (if using) and water into a large bowl and mix to a soft pliable dough (add a little extra water if necessary). Tip out onto a lightly floured surface and knead for 5–6 minutes until you have a very smooth dough, then put the dough back in the bowl and leave to rest for 1 hour.
250 g/9 oz strong white flour, plus extra for dusting	
1 tablespoon salt	
30 g/1 oz yeast	
50 g/2 oz butter (optional)	
300 ml/½ pint water	Line a baking tray. Incorporate the sunflower seeds into the dough, then shape the dough into a ball and flatten with your hands. Using a knife, make vertical slashes around the sides of the dough, from top to bottom, then roll the dough in any remaining seeds. Put onto the baking tray and leave to rise in a warm place for 1 hour.
150 g/5 oz sunflower seeds	
Makes 1 loaf	

Preheat the oven to 220°C/425°F/ mark 7. Bake the loaf for 30 minutes until golden brown, then transfer to a wire rack to cool.

Rye with Caraway

300 g/11 oz rye flour, plus extra for dusting	Put half the rye flour, half the white flour and all the yeast into a large bowl, then add about 175 ml/6 fl oz of water and mix well until you have a thick paste. Leave this dough in the bowl overnight for 10–12 hours.
200 g/7 oz strong white flour, plus extra for dusting	
30 g/1 oz yeast	
300 ml/½ pint water	
1½ teaspoons salt	Add the rest of the flours, the salt, butter, caraway seeds and remaining water and mix well in the bowl for 3 minutes. Tip out onto a lightly floured surface and knead well for 3 minutes, then put the dough back in the bowl and leave to rise for 1 hour.
60 g/2½ oz butter, softened	
60 g/2½ oz caraway seeds	
Makes 1 loaf	

Line a baking tray. Tip the dough out onto your floured surface and roll into a ball, then, using a rolling pin, flatten it slightly into a disc. Cover the top with rye flour, put the dough on the baking tray and leave to rise for 2 hours.

Preheat the oven to 220°C/425°F/ mark 7. Bake the loaf for 30 minutes, then serve warm with smoked salmon.

Fruit and Nut Breads

This bread was one of the first breads I made when I worked at the Chester Grosvenor Hotel. It was produced for the restaurant and went well with the cheeseboard. It's a real old favourite.

You can also make this bread with 100 per cent white flour. This will give a slightly different texture.

Stilton and Walnut Wholemeal Loaf

100 g/3½ oz strong white flour, plus extra for dusting

400 g/14 oz wholemeal flour

1 tablespoon salt

30 g/1 oz yeast

50 g/2 oz butter, softened

300 ml/½ pint water

100 g/3½ oz Stilton cheese, crumbled

125 g/4 oz walnuts, chopped

Makes 1 loaf

Put the flours, salt, yeast and butter into a bowl. Add the water, a little at a time, and gradually incorporate all the flour from the sides of the bowl.

Turn the dough out onto a lightly floured surface and knead for 5 minutes until the dough is smooth and pliable. Put back in the bowl and leave to rise for 1 hour.

Line a baking tray. Add the Stilton and walnuts to the dough and mix well together. Divide the dough into three pieces and roll each one into a long sausage. Plait the dough – place the three strips side by side and join them at the top, then bring the right strip over the middle strip, then the left strip over, and continue until the plait is complete. Put on the tray and leave to rise for 1 hour.

Preheat the oven to 230°C/450°F/mark 8. Bake the loaf for 30 minutes then transfer to a wire rack to cool.

Made on Good Friday, this bread is eaten throughout the Easter weekend, so you can throw the chocolates away.

This is a moist, chewy bread packed with goodness. For me it's a breakfast bread, but it would be equally at home on a cheeseboard.

Fruit Bread

Date and Fig Bread *Illustrated*

500 g/1 lb 2 oz strong white flour, plus extra for dusting

1 tablespoon salt

30 g/1 oz yeast

75 g/3 oz caster sugar

75 g/3 oz butter, softened

3 medium eggs, beaten

300 ml/½ pint milk and water mixed

1 tablespoon ground cinnamon

50 g/2 oz mandarin segments

75 g/3 oz sultanas

60 g/2½ oz mixed peel

zest of 3 lemons

zest of 3 oranges

Makes 2 loaves

Put the flour, salt, yeast, sugar, butter and eggs into a large bowl. Gradually add the milk and water mixture and bind the ingredients together for 3 minutes. Tip the dough out onto a lightly floured surface and knead for 5 minutes, then put the dough back in the bowl and leave for 1½ hours to rise.

Line a baking tray. Incorporate the cinnamon, mandarins, sultanas, mixed peel and zests into the dough, then divide the dough into two pieces and shape each into a ball. Flatten the balls to about 7.5 cm/3 inches thick, then, using a knife, score each piece into eight equal segments. Place the dough on the baking tray and leave to rise for 1 hour.

Preheat the oven to 220°C/425°F/ mark 7. Bake the breads for 20 minutes until golden brown, then transfer to a wire rack to cool.

400 g/14 oz wholemeal flour

100 g/3½ oz strong white flour, plus extra for dusting

1 tablespoon salt

30 g/1 oz yeast

50 g/2 oz butter, softened

1 tablespoon treacle

300 ml/½ pint water

75 g/3 oz dried figs, chopped

75 g/3 oz dates, chopped

Makes 2 small loaves

Put the flours, salt, yeast, butter, treacle and water into a bowl and mix for 5 minutes. Tip out onto a lightly floured surface and knead for 5 minutes, then put the dough back in the bowl and leave for 1 hour to rise.

Line a baking tray. Incorporate the figs and dates into the dough, then divide it into two pieces. Shape the pieces into balls, place on the baking tray and leave to rise for 1 hour.

Preheat the oven to 220°C/425°F/ mark 7. Dust the loaves with flour and, using a knife, make three equidistant horizontal cuts all around each ball. Bake for 30 minutes, then transfer to a wire rack to cool.

This bread was inspired by a friend of mine, Chris Davies, an avid cook who wanted an unusual bread for his dinner guests. I think it did the trick!

John Woods, the Executive Chef at the Cliveden hotel, asked me to make a bread to complement his new cheeseboard, so after various experiments I came up with this one. Its sweet, slightly nutty flavour is delicious with Stilton and the stronger French cheeses – try it as a starter topped with baked Camembert and cranberries.

Grape and Sultana Bread

Date, Prune and Pecan Bread *Illustrated*

500 g/1 lb 2 oz strong white flour, plus extra for dusting

1½ teaspoons salt

30 g/1 oz caster sugar

30 g/1 oz yeast, crumbled

30 g/1 oz butter, softened

300 ml/½ pint water

75 g/3 oz red seedless grapes

75 g/3 oz sultanas

Makes 1 loaf

Put the flour, salt, sugar, yeast and butter into a large bowl and mix together, then slowly add the water until all the flour has been incorporated (you might not need all of it). Tip out onto a lightly floured surface and, using your fingers and palms, knead for 5 minutes. Put the bread back in the bowl and leave to rest for 1 hour.

Line a baking tray. Add the grapes and sultanas to the dough and mix in well, then shape into a ball, flatten slightly using your hand and dust the top with flour. Put onto the baking tray and leave to rise for 1 hour.

Preheat the oven to 200°C/400°F/ mark 6. Cut a square in the top of the dough and bake for 25 minutes. Transfer to a wire rack to cool.

15 g/½ oz yeast

500 g/1 lb 2 oz wholemeal flour, plus extra for dusting

2 teaspoons salt

50 g/2 oz butter, softened

water to mix

125 g/4 oz pecans, chopped

150 g/5 oz dates, chopped

40 g/1½ oz soft, ready-to-eat dried prunes, chopped

Makes 2 x 450 g/ 1lb loaves

Dilute the yeast in a little warm water, then put with the flour, salt and butter into a bowl and mix well. Slowly add enough water, mixing all the time, until the dough becomes elastic. Tip out onto a lightly floured surface and knead the dough for 5 minutes. Put the dough back in the bowl and leave to rest for 2 hours.

Divide the dough into two pieces and incorporate half the pecans, dates and prunes into each piece, pressing in firmly. Knead for a further 5 minutes, then rest the loaves for 1 hour.

Preheat the oven to 200°C/400°F/ mark 6. Grease two 450 g/1 lb loaf tins. Flatten each loaf and roll into a sausage shape. Place the seam underneath, then taper each end. Put each loaf into a tin, seam-side down, dust with flour and, using a knife, cut a zigzag pattern on the top. Bake for 25–30 minutes, then turn out onto a wire rack to cool.

This bread is a must on any cheeseboard. I would suggest serving it with a ripe Stilton or, failing that, try it with the creamy Savoyard cheese Reblochon – oh, and a glass of red wine.

This bread was originally made while I was head baker at the Dorchester Hotel in London. It was baked for the breakfast menu, but quickly made its way to the cheese trolley – it's great with most cheeses.

Walnut Bread

Walnut and Sultana Bread

350 g/12 oz wholemeal flour

150 g/5 oz strong white flour, plus extra for dusting

1½ teaspoons salt

30 g/1 oz yeast

40 g/1½ oz butter, softened

60 ml/2 fl oz walnut oil

300 ml/½ pint water

150 g/5 oz walnut pieces

Makes 1 loaf

Put all the ingredients except the walnuts into a large bowl, then mix well with your hands for 4 minutes. When all the flour has been incorporated, tip the dough out onto a lightly floured surface and, using your fingers and the heel of your palm, knead for 5 minutes. Put the dough back in the bowl and leave to rise for 1 hour.

Line a baking tray. Incorporate the walnuts into the dough, shape into a ball and dust with white flour. Place on the baking tray and leave to rise for 1 hour.

Preheat the oven to 220°C/425°F/ mark 7. Using a sharp knife, cut a cross into the top of the dough, then bake the bread for 30 minutes until golden. Transfer to a wire rack to cool.

400 g/14 oz wholemeal flour

100 g/3½ oz strong white flour, plus extra for dusting

1 tablespoon salt

30 g/1 oz yeast

60 g/2½ oz butter, softened

300 ml/½ pint water

125 g/4 oz walnut pieces

100 g/3½ oz sultanas

Makes 1 loaf

Put all the ingredients except the water, walnuts and sultanas into a bowl, then slowly add the water and, using your hands, bind the ingredients together. When all the flour has been incorporated, tip the dough out onto a lightly floured surface and, using your fingers and the heel of your palm, knead for 5 minutes. Put the dough back in the bowl and leave to rise for 2 hours.

Line a baking tray. Incorporate the walnuts and sultanas into the dough, shape into a ball and make a hole in the middle with your finger. Slowly begin to open the hole until it is about 5 cm/ 2 inches across. Dust with white flour, place on the baking tray and leave to rise for 1 hour.

Preheat the oven to 230°C/450°F/ mark 8. Bake the bread for 30 minutes until golden, then transfer to a wire rack to cool. Serve with cheese, or at breakfast toasted, with butter.

This is a very German way of making rye bread and the apricot adds a lovely fruity kick to an already fantastic loaf. You need to start this the day before.

Apricot Rye

300 g/11 oz rye flour, plus extra for dusting

200 g/7 oz strong white flour, plus extra for dusting

30 g/1 oz yeast

345 ml/12 fl oz water

1½ teaspoons salt

60 g/2½ oz butter, softened

125 g/4 oz dried apricots, chopped

Makes 1 loaf

Put half the rye flour, half the white flour and all the yeast into a bowl. Then add about 175 ml/6 fl oz of water and mix well until you have a thick paste. Leave this overnight for 10–12 hours.

Add the rest of the flours and water, the salt, butter and apricots to the dough and mix well for 3 minutes, then tip out onto a lightly floured surface and knead well for 3 minutes. Put the dough back in the bowl and leave to rise for 1 hour.

Line a baking tray. Shape the dough into a sausage and taper the ends. Place on the baking tray and leave to rise for 1 hour.

Preheat the oven to 230°C/450°F/mark 8. Rub rye flour all over the top of the dough and, using a knife, cut zigzags down the centre of the loaf. Bake in the oven for 30 minutes, then transfer to a wire rack to cool.

An incredibly luxurious bread that will be eaten in one sitting. IF there is any left, use it to make extra-rich bread and butter pudding. This is definitely not a bread to count calories with!

Chocolate and Sour Cherry Bread

500 g/1 lb 2 oz strong white flour, plus extra for dusting

2 teaspoons salt

30 ml/1 fl oz olive oil

15 g/½ oz yeast

warm water to mix

160 g tin black cherries, drained

200 g packet chocolate chips

Makes 2 loaves

Put the flour into a bowl with the salt, olive oil and yeast. Slowly add the warm water and mix by hand until the dough is pliable.

Tip the dough out onto a lightly floured surface and knead for 4–7 minutes. Put the dough back in the bowl and leave to rest for 1 hour.

Line a baking tray. Divide the dough into two pieces and add half the cherries to each one. (You may need to add a little more flour if the mix becomes too sloppy.) Now add half the chocolate chips to each dough. Mix well, adding a little flour if the dough becomes too soft. Shape the dough into 2 balls and flatten to about 5 cm/2 inches high. Dust heavily with flour and score diagonal lines across the top to form diamond shapes. Place on the baking tray and leave the dough to rest for 1 hour.

Preheat the oven to 200°C/400°F/mark 6. Bake the bread for 20–25 minutes, then transfer to a wire rack to cool.

This is comfort food at its best – rich and filling. Eat it toasted for tea, dripping with butter or, better still, piled high with baked apples or peaches with a dollop of fresh vanilla ice cream on top.

Banana and Muesli Bread

500 g/1 lb 2 oz wholemeal flour

2 teaspoons salt

15 g/½ oz yeast

50 g/2 oz butter, softened

320 ml/11 fl oz water

2 large bananas, chopped

1 bowl of muesli

Makes 2 loaves

Put the flour, salt, yeast and butter into a bowl. Slowly add water to the bowl and mix carefully by hand until the dough becomes elastic. Knead the dough for 5 minutes, then cover the bowl and set aside to rest for 2 hours.

Divide the dough into two, then add a chopped banana to each, using your hands to 'mash' the banana into the mixture. Your dough will now be sticky, so add enough muesli to each to regain the original texture.

Line a baking tray. Roll each dough into a ball, then press into the bowl of muesli, so that the dough becomes completely coated. Place the loaves on the baking tray and leave to rise for 1–2 hours.

Preheat the oven to 200°C/400°F/mark 6. Using a knife, deeply score the top of each ball into 8 sections. Bake the loaves for 25–30 minutes, then transfer to a wire rack to cool.

I was inspired to make this bread when I visited a small artisan bakery in Tours (Loire), France. The baker produced a bread with oranges, saffron and honey made from a traditional recipe favoured by famous local poet François Rabelais. My twist was to try it with oranges and lemons – I think it works well.

Toasted with butter – perfect.

Lemon and Orange Bread

400 g/14 oz strong white flour, plus extra for dusting

100 g/3½ oz rye flour

1 tablespoon salt

60 g/2½ oz butter, softened

60 g/2½ oz caster sugar

30 g/1 oz yeast

300 ml/½ pint water

zest of 5 lemons

zest of 6 oranges

Makes 2 small loaves or 1 large loaf

Put the flours, salt, butter, sugar, yeast and water into a bowl and massage the dough together with your hands for 3 minutes. Then tip the dough out onto a lightly floured surface, add the zests and work them well into the dough: the dough will discolour slightly, but don't worry. Put the dough back in the bowl and leave to rise for 1 hour.

Line a baking tray. If making two loaves, divide the dough into two equal pieces. Shape the dough(s) into a ball shape and push your finger down through the middle until you can feel the table underneath. Then, using a sharp knife, cut them across the top several times, place on the baking tray and leave to rise for 1 hour.

Preheat the oven to 220°C/425°F/mark 7. Bake for 25 minutes until golden brown, then transfer to a wire rack to cool.

Orange, Lemon and Cherry Bread

500 g/1 lb 2 oz strong white flour, plus extra for dusting

1 tablespoon salt

30 g/1 oz caster sugar

40 g/1½ oz butter, softened

30 g/1 oz yeast

zest of 1 lemon

zest of 3 oranges

300 ml/½ pint water

75 g/3 oz morello cherries

Makes 1 loaf

Put all the ingredients except the cherries into a bowl and mix to a dough. Tip the dough out onto a lightly floured surface and knead for 5 minutes, then put the dough back into the bowl and leave to rest for 1 hour.

Line a baking tray. Add the cherries to the dough and mix well, then divide the dough into two pieces and roll each out to about 30.5 cm/12 inches long. Twist the two pieces together and place on the baking tray, then leave to rise for 1 hour.

Preheat the oven to 200°C/400°F/mark 6. Bake the bread for 25 minutes, then transfer to a wire rack to cool.

The subtle flavours and smells in this bread are unique. Saffron works well with dough, but you could also try mango chutney – just replace the saffron with 75 g/3 oz of the chutney: yummy!

Honey and Saffron Loaf

250 g/9 oz strong white flour

250 g/9 oz wholemeal flour

30 g/1 oz yeast

300 ml/½ pint water

1 tablespoon salt

75 ml/3 fl oz honey

2 small boxes saffron, diluted in a little water

Makes 1 loaf

Put half the white flour, half the wholemeal flour and all the yeast into a bowl and add 150 ml/¼ pint of water. Whisk together and mix for 5 minutes, then leave for 4 hours.

Add the remaining flours and water, the salt, honey and saffron to the dough and knead well for 5 minutes. Leave in the bowl to rest for 30 minutes.

Line a baking tray. Shape the dough into a ball, place on the tray and leave to rise for 1 hour.

Preheat the oven to 220°C/425°F/mark 7. Score around the middle of the loaf with a knife and bake for 30 minutes. Transfer to a wire rack to cool.

This bread is always a great favourite with the kids at teatime, loaded with honey or chocolate spread. For a change, serve it with cream cheese and celery as an energy-giving sandwich.

Peanut Bread

500 g/1 lb 2 oz strong white flour

1½ teaspoons salt

15 g/½ oz yeast

warm water to mix

¾ jar of crunchy peanut butter

100 g/3½ oz caramelized peanut chips, to mix

Makes 2 loaves

Put the flour, salt and yeast into a bowl. Slowly add warm water and mix by hand until the dough is pliable. Leave in the bowl to rest for 1 hour.

Add the peanut butter to the dough and mix it in thoroughly. The dough will now be sticky, so begin to add the peanut chips until the dough tightens up again. Divide the dough into two pieces and leave to rest for 1 hour.

Grease a baking tray. Punch any air out of the dough pieces and mould into two sausage shapes, approx. 30.5 cm/12 inches long and tapering at each end. Roll them up into a coil, place them on the baking tray and leave to prove for 1 hour.

Preheat the oven to 200°C/400°F/mark 6. Using a sharp knife, score a line down the middle of each loaf and dust each lightly with flour. Bake the loaves for 20–25 minutes, then transfer to a wire rack to cool.

A bread I devised while I was in Cyprus; it's gorgeous toasted and with lashings of butter.

Almond Bread

500 g/1 lb 2 oz strong white flour

1 tablespoon salt

60 g/2½ oz caster sugar

40 g/1½ oz butter, softened

75 g/3 oz ground almonds

30 g/1 oz yeast

300 ml/½ pint milk and water mixed

125 g/4 oz flaked almonds

Makes 1 loaf

Put the flour, salt, sugar, butter, ground almonds and yeast into a bowl. Add the milk and water mix and blend for 2 minutes. Tip out of the bowl onto a lightly floured surface and knead with your hands until the dough becomes soft and pliable. This should take no more than 5 minutes. Put the dough back in the bowl and leave to rise for 1 hour.

Line a baking tray. Tip the dough out onto your floured surface and mix in half the flaked almonds. Flatten the dough into an oval shape and cover the outside of the dough with the remaining flaked almonds. Place the dough on the baking tray and leave to rise for 1 hour.

Preheat the oven to 220°C/425°F/mark 7. Bake the bread for 20–25 minutes, then transfer to a wire rack to cool.

My wife's favourite Danish. Remember Valentine's Day – get baking. Probably you won't use all the pastries at once, so you can freeze the finished dough for up to 3 months. You need to start this the day before.

Apple and Sultana Danish Pastries

For the pastry

20 g/¾ oz yeast

625 g/1 lb 7 oz strong white flour, plus extra for dusting

1½ teaspoons salt

75 g/3 oz caster sugar

water to mix

500 g/1 lb 2 oz butter, chilled

For the filling

10 apples, peeled and cored

100 g/3½ oz sultanas

2 teaspoons ground cinnamon

2 eggs, beaten, for eggwash

apricot jam, warmed, to glaze

For the water icing

lemon zest, icing sugar and water

Makes about 30 Danish pastries

Dilute the yeast in a little warm water and put with the flour, salt and sugar into a large mixing bowl. Using a wooden spoon, slowly mix in a little water until the dough becomes pliable. Tip the dough out onto a lightly floured surface and knead well until it feels elastic. Put the dough back in the bowl and leave in the fridge for 1 hour.

Return the chilled dough to your floured work surface and roll it into a rectangle 60 x 30.5 cm/24 x12 inches. Flatten the chilled butter into a rectangle about 1 cm/½ inch thick and lay it over two-thirds of the dough. Bring the uncovered third of the dough into the centre, then fold the covered top third down, so that your dough is now in three layers. Return the dough to the fridge to chill for 1 hour.

Scatter some more flour over your table and roll out the dough to the same-sized rectangle as before. Repeat the folding process, one side on top of the other, and place the dough back in the fridge for 1 hour. You will need to repeat this process twice more before leaving the dough to rest, wrapped in clingfilm, overnight.

Line a baking tray. Roll out the dough to about 5 mm/¼ inch thick, then cut 12.5 cm/5 inch squares from the dough. Fold the edges into the middle so you have a parcel, place each one onto the baking tray and leave to rise for 2 hours at an ambient temperature (20°C+).

Meanwhile, cook the apples in a pan with a little water to soften them for 7 minutes, then add the sultanas and cinnamon and allow to cool.

Spoon at least 2 tablespoons of the apple mixture into the middle of each dough square. Preheat the oven to 200°C/400°F/mark 6. Brush the eggwash onto the exposed parts of the dough, and bake for 20 minutes. Take out of the oven and brush with warmed apricot jam. Cool, then top with water icing (see page 124).

Once you've prepared the dough and cut out the shapes you can freeze them for use later, if you wish.

This was a favourite of mine at the Cliveden hotel in the morning, eaten with a cup of tea, while sitting by the window looking at the view across the grounds.

Strawberry Danish

Pain au Raisin Danish Pastries *Illustrated*

1 quantity Danish Pastry dough (see page 121)

For the filling

1 punnet of strawberries, quartered

270 ml/9 fl oz extra-thick strawberry yoghurt

1 tin thick custard

1 egg, beaten, for eggwash

1 packet flaked almonds

2 dessertspoons apricot jam

Makes 30–40 Danish pastries

Make the pastry as on page 121, up to the point where it is chilled overnight. Roll out to 3 mm/⅛ inch thick and cut into 30.5 cm/12 inch long by 12.5 cm/5 inch wide pieces. If you find that you don't have enough for these lengths don't worry, make the lengths 20.5 or 15 cm/8 or 6 inches long.

Line several baking trays. Add the strawberries to the yoghurt and fold in the custard. Spoon some of this mixture down the middle of each of the long rectangles and fold in half lengthways. Using a knife, cut lines into the dough widthways about 10 cm/4 inches apart all the way along. Brush with the eggwash and sprinkle the flaked almonds all over the tops. Put the dough on the baking trays and leave to rise for 1 hour.

Preheat the oven to 200°C/400°F/mark 6. Bake the Danish for 20 minutes until golden brown. Transfer to a wire rack to cool, then cut into fingers along the width.

Put the apricot jam in a small saucepan with a splash of water and bring up to boil. Brush this onto the Danish pastries and serve.

1 quantity Danish Pastry dough (see page 121)

For the filling

100 g/3½ oz fresh custard

250 g/9 oz raisins or sultanas

1½ teaspoons cinnamon

1 egg, beaten, for eggwash

100 g/3½ oz apricot jam

For the water icing

lemon zest, icing sugar and water

Makes 40–50 Danish pastries

Make the pastry as on page 121, up to the point where it is chilled overnight.

Using a rolling pin, flatten the dough into a rectangle 3 mm/⅛ inch thick. Spread the custard over the top and sprinkle liberally with raisins or sultanas, add a sprinkle of cinnamon and roll the dough up into a sausage. Line several baking trays. Cut the sausage into 2.5 cm/1 inch pieces, place flat-side down on the baking trays and leave to rise for 1½ hours.

Preheat the oven to 200°C/400°F/mark 6. Brush the Danish lightly with the eggwash and bake for 10–15 minutes until golden brown. Transfer to a wire rack and brush with warm apricot jam. Leave to cool, then top with water icing (see page 124).

This bread reminds me of a little bakery near to where I was brought up in Merseyside. On my way back from school I would buy a Sally Lunn and eat it with butter when I got home.

124 Sally Lunns

400 g/14 oz strong white flour, plus extra for dusting

1½ teaspoons salt

40 g/1½ oz caster sugar

40 g/1½ oz butter, softened

30 g/1 oz yeast

120 ml/4 fl oz milk

120 ml/4 fl oz water, plus extra for icing

50 g/2 oz sultanas

60 g/2½ oz glacé cherries

1 teaspoon ground cinnamon

zest of 3 oranges

75 g/3 oz icing sugar

Makes 1 loaf

Put the flour, salt, sugar, butter, yeast, milk and water into a bowl and mix together with your hands. When all the flour has been incorporated tip the dough out onto a lightly floured surface and knead until smooth and pliable. Put the dough back in the bowl and leave for 1 hour to rest.

Line a baking tray. Add the sultanas, cherries, cinnamon and orange zest to the dough and, using an electric mixer (blade attachment) or your hands, work it in well. Shape the dough into a sausage shape by flattening out the dough and rolling it up. Place the dough on the baking tray and leave to rise for 1 hour.

Preheat the oven to 200°C/400°F/mark 6. Bake the dough for 20 minutes, then transfer to a wire rack to cool.

While it is cooling, make a water icing. Tip the icing sugar into a bowl, add a little water and mix in well, then gradually add water until the icing coats the back of a spoon. Drizzle the icing over the top of the bread. Cut into slices and eat with lashings of butter.

These are great toasted, with butter.

Teacakes

400 g/14 oz
strong white flour,
plus extra for dusting

1½ teaspoons salt

40 g/1½ oz caster
sugar

1 teaspoon ground
cinnamon

50 g/2 oz butter,
softened

30 g/1 oz yeast

200 ml/7½ fl oz water

75 g/3 oz sultanas

60 g/2½ oz mixed peel

1 egg, beaten,
for eggwash

Makes 10–15

Put the flour, salt, sugar, cinnamon, butter, yeast and water into a large bowl and mix together for 2 minutes. Tip the dough out onto a lightly floured surface and knead for 5 minutes, then put back into the bowl and leave for 1 hour to rest.

Line a baking tray. Add the sultanas and mixed peel to the dough and divide the dough into 75 g/3 oz pieces. Shape each piece into a ball and, using a rolling pin, flatten them out to 2.5 cm/1 inch thick. Place the teacakes on the baking tray and leave to rise for 1 hour.

Preheat the oven to 190°C/375°F/mark 5. Brush the teacakes with eggwash and bake for 15 minutes.

I wanted to go back to the way we used to make Hot Cross Buns, using real fruit rather than all dried. The result is this juicy bun – the kids will love it, and adults will too!

Hollywood Hot Cross Buns

500 g/1 lb 2 oz strong white flour, plus extra for dusting

1½ teaspoons salt

75 g/3 oz caster sugar

50 g/2 oz yeast

300 ml/½ pint milk and water mixed

60 g/2½ oz mandarin segments, chopped

60 g/2½ oz peach slices, chopped

60 g/2½ oz apple slices, chopped

2 teaspoons ground cinnamon

60 g/2½ oz apricot jam, warmed, to glaze

For the crosses

200 ml/7 fl oz water

200 g/7 oz flour

2 medium eggs

Makes 15–20

Put the flour, salt, sugar and yeast into a bowl. Slowly add enough of the milk and water mix to achieve a pliable dough. Tip out onto a lightly floured surface and knead well for 5 minutes, then put the dough back in the bowl and leave to rise for 1 hour.

Incorporate the mandarins, peaches, apples and cinnamon into the dough and leave to rise for 1 hour.

Line a baking tray. Divide the dough into 75 g/3 oz pieces and roll each into a ball. Put them on the baking tray and leave to rest for 1 hour.

Preheat the oven to 200°C/400°F/mark 6. To make the crosses, whisk together the water, flour and eggs to a smooth paste and pipe a cross on top of each bun. Bake the buns for 25 minutes until golden brown. Take out of the oven and brush them with warmed apricot jam. Serve immediately.

An obvious treat for my son Joshua, and a favourite of mine when I'm watching a video on those cold winter days.

Doughnuts

250 g/9 oz strong white flour, plus extra for dusting

pinch of salt

40 g/1½ oz caster sugar

30 g/1 oz butter, softened

150 ml/¼ pint water

20 g/¾ oz yeast

vegetable or sunflower oil for frying

caster sugar, to coat

Makes 5–10

Put all the ingredients except the oil and coating sugar into a large bowl and mix together, then tip out onto a lightly floured surface and knead for 5 minutes. Put the dough back in the bowl and leave to double in size.

Divide the dough into 75 g/3 oz pieces and shape into balls. Put on your floured surface and leave to rise until doubled in size.

Pour some vegetable or sunflower oil into a large heavy-based pan and heat to 170°C/325°F, or a medium heat. Lower each of the doughnuts into the oil and fry until brown, then roll them over and fry the other side. (If you have a problem with rolling the doughnuts over then pierce them slightly with a knife.) The frying should take no more than 5 minutes for both sides. When they are browned, tip them straight into a bowl full of caster sugar and coat well. Cool them on a wire rack, then enjoy with a nice cup of tea.

Sweet Treats

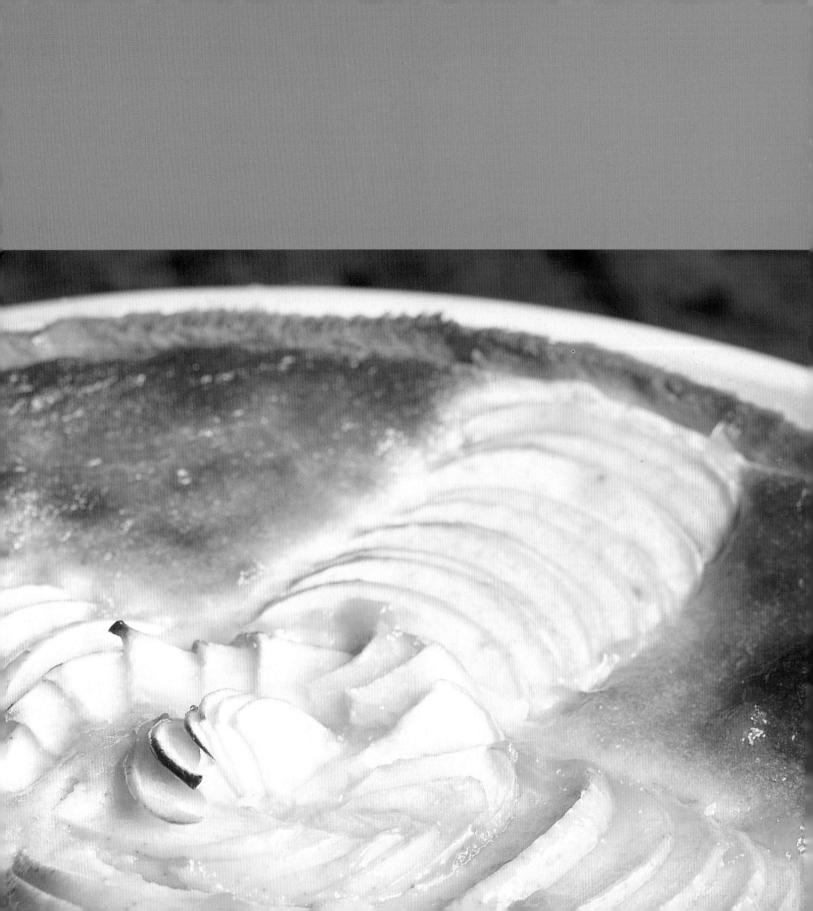

This has to be the easiest ice cream to make and it is absolutely delicious. Serve it stuffed into baked pears or peaches or as a sweet pancake filling – unbelievable!

This has the edge over traditional bread and butter pudding – the buttery croissants and tartness of the blueberries really lifts this dish.

Brown Bread Ice Cream

Croissant Pudding

75 g/3 oz brown breadcrumbs (from Guinness and Treacle Bread, page 28)

60 g/2½ oz brown sugar

3 large eggs, separated

1 tablespoon dark rum

270 ml/9 fl oz double cream

75 g/3 oz icing sugar

Serves 4–6

Mix the breadcrumbs and brown sugar together, then place on a baking tray and grill for 8 minutes or until dark and caramelized. When the mixture is cool, break up into small, bite-sized pieces.

Whisk the egg whites until stiff. In a separate bowl, mix the egg yolks with the rum, then fold this mixture into the egg whites. Finally, whisk the cream and icing sugar together, then, using a metal spoon, fold the cream and breadcrumbs into the egg mixture. Pour into a metal container and freeze for about 4 hours before serving.

12 butter croissants (see page 48)

75 g/3 oz blackberries, plus a few extra to serve

75 g/3 oz blueberries, plus a few extra to serve

75 g/3 oz raspberries, plus a few extra to serve

splash of kirsch

icing sugar

For the sauce Anglaise

400 ml/14 fl oz milk

2 vanilla pods

3 medium eggs

40 g/1½ oz caster sugar

Serves 6

Preheat the oven to 180°C/350°F/ mark 4. Cut the croissants lengthways and place in a large casserole dish. Sprinkle over the berries and add a splash of kirsch.

To make the sauce Anglaise, put the milk and vanilla pods in a pan and bring to the boil. Whisk the eggs and sugar together to a froth, then pour the milk onto the eggs and return to the pan. Boil for 6 minutes to reduce, then pour over the croissants in the casserole dish.

Bake in the oven for 30 minutes. Take out of the oven, sprinkle with icing sugar and caramelize with a blow torch or under the grill. Serve with pouring cream and more berries.

I made this recipe for Easter some years back. It appeals to both children and adults alike.

Savarin with Chocolate Sauce and Eggs

For the savarin

450 g/1 lb strong white flour

175 ml/6 fl oz milk

50 g/2 oz yeast

pinch of salt

60 g/2½ oz caster sugar

4 medium eggs

200 g/7 oz butter

For the sauce

1 bar milk chocolate, melted

1 carton thick custard

To decorate

apricot jam, warmed, or warm stock syrup (½ sugar to ½ water)

mini chocolate eggs

Serves 8

To make the savarin, put all the ingredients into a bowl and mix together. Beat well for 6 minutes until smooth, then place in a savarin ring and leave to rise for 1 hour until light to touch.

Preheat the oven to 200°C/400°F/mark 6. Bake the savarin for 25 minutes until golden brown.

Meanwhile, make the chocolate sauce by stirring the melted chocolate into the custard.

Tip the savarin out of the ring and brush with the warm apricot jam or stock syrup, if using. Fill the centre with chocolate sauce and top with mini eggs.

These muffins are great eaten warm and covered with pouring cream, or serve them cold as a snack. Either way they're a winner.

Blueberry Muffins *Illustrated*

250 g/9 oz butter, softened

185 g/6½ oz caster sugar

4 medium eggs

250 g/9 oz strong white flour

1½ teaspoons baking powder

16 paper muffin cases

2 punnets blueberries

icing sugar, for dusting

Makes 16 muffins

Preheat the oven to 200°C/400°F/ mark 6. Cream the butter and sugar until white and fluffy, then add the eggs and mix for a further 5 minutes. Sift in the flour and baking powder and mix into a smooth paste.

Line your muffin tray with the paper cases and drop a spoonful of the mixture into each case. Gently press the blueberries into the centre of each muffin.

Bake for 12 minutes or until a muffin springs back when pressed. Transfer to a wire rack to cool, then dust lightly with icing sugar.

These muffins are just spectacular served at teatime with a dollop of clotted cream, preferably accompanying cucumber sandwiches and a cup of Earl Grey tea – anyone for tennis?

Wimbledon Muffins

250 g/9 oz butter, softened

185 g/6½ oz caster sugar

5 medium eggs

250 g/9 oz strong white flour

1½ teaspoons baking powder

16 paper muffin cases

16 medium-size strawberries, each sliced into 3

icing sugar, for dusting

Makes 16 muffins

Preheat the oven to 200°C/400°F/ mark 6. Cream the butter and sugar until white and fluffy, then add the eggs and mix for a further 5 minutes. Sift in the flour and baking powder and mix into a smooth paste.

Line your muffin tray with the paper cases and drop a spoonful of the mixture into each one. Gently press the sliced strawberries into the centre of each muffin.

Bake for 12 minutes or until a muffin springs back when pressed. Transfer to a wire rack to cool, then dust lightly with icing sugar.

I've included pancakes in this book mainly because they contain flour and when I was working in hotels these recipes, along with some tarts and pies, were still under the jurisdiction of the baker rather than the pastry chef.

This recipe is very simple to make and the pancakes are delicious served on a bed of cream with raspberry sauce rippled through it.

Pancakes with Bananas and Cream

250 g/8 oz white flour

30 g/1 oz caster sugar

1 egg

200 ml/7½ fl oz milk

60 ml/2½ fl oz sunflower oil

20 g/¾ oz butter

2 bananas, chopped

1 tablespoon dark rum

200 ml/7½ fl oz whipped cream

Serves 2

Whisk together the flour, 20 g/¾ oz of the sugar, the egg and milk for 5 minutes. You should now have a batter mixture. Test it by dipping a spoon in and seeing if it coats the back of the spoon evenly.

Heat a little sunflower oil in a frying pan and leave to smoke, then pour half a cup of the batter in the middle of the pan, tilt the pan to move the batter to the edges and replace on the heat for 3 minutes. Turn the pancake over with a spatula and fry for another 2 minutes. Remove from the pan and put on a plate to cool. Repeat with the rest of the batter.

To make the filling, drop the butter into the frying pan, add the bananas and cook for 1 minute. Add the rum and flambé until the flames die down. Cook for a further 2 minutes and leave to the side.

Whisk up the cream with the remaining sugar and spoon a little into the middle of each pancake. Top with the bananas, roll up and serve on a pool of pouring cream, if so desired – watch those waistlines!

My father and mother were both excellent at making pastry and I grew up knowing how to make good sweet pastry. Some pastry work is essential to becoming a good baker – it gives you a little edge on the competition.

I had this tart in Chinon in the Loire with a glass of Chablis for lunch, delicious!

Normandy Apple Tart

For the paste

375 g/13 oz strong white flour, plus extra for dusting

250 g/9 oz caster sugar

125 g/4 oz butter, softened

1 medium egg

splash of water to mix

4 dessert apples, thinly sliced

100 g/3½ oz apricot jam, warmed

For the frangipane

200 g/7 oz butter, softened

200 g/7 oz caster sugar

2 medium eggs plus 2 medium egg yolks

splash of calvados

60 g/2½ oz flour

200 g/7 oz ground almonds

Serves 8

Preheat the oven to 200°C/400°F/mark 6. To make the sweet paste, put the flour, sugar, butter, egg and water into a bowl and combine. Roll out on a lightly floured surface and use to line a 30.5 cm/12 inch shallow round cake tin.

To make the frangipane, cream the butter and sugar together and add the eggs and egg yolks one at a time. Add the Calvados, flour and ground almonds and mix well. Spread the frangipane over the paste in the cake ring, then fan out the apple slices from the edge to the middle in the form of a cross.

Bake for 25 minutes until golden brown. Brush with apricot jam while still warm and serve immediately.

My twist on the traditional recipe. The addition of real fruit lifts the
pies to new heights. Remember when lining the moulds to keep the
pastry thin and add plenty of filling.

Hollywood Mince Pies

For the pastry

**375 g/13 oz strong
white flour**

**250 g/9 oz butter,
softened**

**125 g/4 oz
caster sugar, plus
extra for sprinkling**

1 medium egg

splash of water to mix

For the filling

2 jars mincemeat

**½ large tin of
mandarins, drained
and chopped**

2 apples, finely diced

Makes 25 pies

Preheat the oven to 200°C/400°F/mark 6. To make the sweet pastry,
rub the flour, butter, sugar and egg together with a splash of water to
make a paste. If using a mixer, use the paddle and mix for 2 minutes.
Do not overmix.

To make the filling, turn the mincemeat out into a bowl, throw the
mandarins and apples into the bowl and blend in by hand.

Use deep muffin moulds. Rip off a small piece of sweet paste and line
the sides and bottom of each mould. Fill each one with a good helping
of the mincemeat mixture so that it reaches three-quarters of the way
up the side of the mould.

Using a rolling pin, roll out your lids and cut to slightly bigger than the
top of the moulds. Place a lid on top of each pie and gently push down.
Prick the lids with a knife and sprinkle with sugar.

Bake for 20 minutes, then transfer to a wire rack to cool. Serve warm
with fresh cream.

A very French recipe my mother-in-law is famous for. The cinnamon really adds another dimension to this pie.

I was first introduced to sweet paste by my mother Gill — she gave me this recipe and it's the best! The pastry will keep, covered in clingfilm, in the fridge for 1 week.

Apple Pie

Apple and Pear Pie with Fruit Sauce *Illustrated*

For the pastry

375 g/13 oz strong white flour

250 g/9 oz caster sugar

125 g/4 oz butter, softened

1 medium egg

100 g/3½ oz ground almonds

For the filling

1.4 kg/3 lb apples, peeled, cored and sliced

splash of Calvados

juice of 3 lemons

handful of sultanas

pinch of cinnamon

For the topping

1 egg, beaten, for eggwash

caster sugar, for sprinkling

Serves 6

Soak the sliced apples in the Calvados and lemon juice for 2 hours. Mix all the pastry ingredients together and leave to rest for 1 hour.

Preheat the oven to 200°C/400°F/ mark 6. Roll out the pastry to fit into a 30.5 cm/12 inch pie tin or foil base and fill with the apples and sultanas. Sprinkle with cinnamon. Roll out the pastry trimmings for the lid, cover the pie and crimp the edges together. Brush with the eggwash and sugar and bake for 25 minutes until golden brown.

For the pastry

375 g/13 oz strong white flour

250 g/9 oz caster sugar

125 g/4 oz butter, softened

1 medium egg

30 ml/1 fl oz water

For the filling

8 apples, peeled, cored and chopped

8 pears, peeled, cored and chopped

40 g/1½ oz sugar

For the topping

1 egg, beaten, for eggwash

caster sugar, for sprinkling

For the sauce

2 punnets raspberries

icing sugar

Serves 6

Preheat the oven to 200°C/400°F/ mark 6. To make the pastry, using a beater on an electric mixer, blend all the ingredients together to make a smooth pastry.

To make the filling, put the fruit and sugar into a pan and cook over a medium heat for 5 minutes to soften the fruit.

Roll the pastry out onto a 30.5 cm/ 12 inch pie plate and spoon on the filling. Roll out the excess pastry to make the lid and place on top. Trim the pastry edges and crimp around the edge, brush with eggwash and sprinkle with sugar. Bake for 25 minutes until golden brown.

Meanwhile make the raspberry sauce. Pass the raspberries through a sieve then stir in a little icing sugar. Serve with the pie.

Index